The Choice of
Orthodoxy

The Choice of
Orthodoxy

The Church—One, Holy, Catholic, and Apostolic

Daniel Daly

ST VLADIMIR'S SEMINARY PRESS

YONKERS, NEW YORK

2023

Publisher's Cataloging-in-Publication
(Provided by Cassidy Cataloguing Services, Inc.).

Names: Daly, Daniel, 1938-
Title: The choice of Orthodoxy : the Church-- one, holy, catholic, and apostolic /
Daniel Daly.
Description: Yonkers, New York : St Vladimir's Seminary Press, 2023. | Includes
bibliographical references.
Identifiers: ISBN: 978-0-88141-749-4 (paperback) | 978-0-88141-750-0 (ebook) | LCCN:
2023939390
Subjects: LCSH: Church history. | Orthodox Eastern Church--History. | Orthodox
Eastern Church-- Doctrines. | Orthodox Eastern Church--Relations--Catholic Church.
| Catholic Church-- History. | Catholic Church--Relations--Orthodox Eastern Church.
| Spirituality-- Christianity. | Christian life. | BISAC: RELIGION / Christian Church /
General. | RELIGION / Christian Church / History. | RELIGION / Christian Living
/ General. | RELIGION / Christian Theology / General. | RELIGION / Christian
Theology / Apologetics. | RELIGION / Christianity / Orthodox. | RELIGION /
Christianity / Catholic. | RELIGION / Spirituality.
Classification: LCC: BX320.3 .D35 2023 | DDC: 281.9--dc23

The source of scriptural quotations, unless otherwise noted, is the *Orthodox Study
Bible*. Specifically, for the Old Testament: Scripture from *The St. Athanasius Academy
Septuagint*™. Copyright © 2008 by St. Athanasius Academy of Orthodox Theology.
Used by permission. All rights reserved. And for the New Testament: Scripture
taken from the New King James Version®. Copyright © 1982 by Thomas Nelson, Inc.
Used by permission. All rights reserved. Any quotation from the King James Version
is marked KJV in the text; the King James Version is in the public domain in the
United States.

Copyright © 2023
St Vladimir's Seminary Press
575 Scarsdale Rd, Yonkers, NY 10707
1–800–204–2665
www.svspress.com

ISBN: 978-0-88141-749-4 (paper)
ISBN: 978-0-88141-750-0 (electronic)

PRINTED IN CANADA

For

Athena Anne

Felicity Sonia

John Roman

The publication of this book was made possible in part by generous donations from Dr Yohannan Abraham, Rev. Dr Corrado Altomare, Charles Makhoul, and Dr Carla Thomas.

Contents

Foreword

So many people today are searching for a spiritual home. In this book, Fr Daniel draws our attention to the plight of contemporary Roman Catholics who feel disconnected from their ancestral Church. He reflects on his personal experience to understand where this feeling of disorientation and rootlessness might come from. He also reflects on social changes that have left many other people—from various religious backgrounds—feeling spiritually homeless and adrift, possibly without even knowing why.

Our Faith is familiar with this feeling. In many respects, this is a Faith of sojourners. In the Bible, we see our first parents, Adam and Eve, evicted from their home in Paradise and all humanity after them wandering this earth in search of a spiritual home. Yet, at the same time, we see God calling people to journey toward a new home that He would provide: He summoned Abraham to venture forth from Ur of the Chaldees to a land He would show him. He led the people of Israel out of Egypt to the Promised Land, flowing with milk and honey. Ultimately, our Lord Jesus Christ revealed the Kingdom of God as the home prepared for us *from the foundation of the world* (Matthew 25.34) and invited all of us to join Him in it.

To this day, we seek this Kingdom, which alone offers the sense of spiritual belonging we desperately need—the peace, joy, and love of a true home. We welcome all earnest seekers to join us on this journey. Together we walk this road, even now experiencing a foretaste of that blessed Kingdom in the life of the Church, while pressing on toward the day when the Kingdom's doors will open wide to all who have pursued it with love and zeal.

I commend Fr Daniel's heartfelt and insightful reflections to all who are searching for such a home. May it be a companion and guide for you, as you seek to reconnect with your Heavenly Father.

+SABA
Archbishop of New York and
Metropolitan of All North America
Antiochian Orthodox Christian
Archdiocese of North America

Acknowledgements

No one is a Christian in isolation. Our life of faith is built upon the witness of countless people: our parents, family, teachers, pastors, and fellow Christians. To them we owe our gratitude. This is certainly true in my life. I owe a personal debt of gratitude to a small group of friends who have assisted me in various ways in the writing of this small book. My friend Mr Tod Mixson, whom I have known for over twenty years, "insisted" that I write the book. Mr Gregory Storey has been a constant source of assistance from the beginning to the end of the book. He provided insights into the content, language, and theology of the book. Two friends offered thoughts that I considered true words of wisdom: Archdeacon David Khorey and Hieromonk Philip Vreeland. The encouragement of former parishioners gave me the determination to complete the work. I thank Dr Charles Makoul,

Dr Frederick Kayal, Rick and Suzanne Merpi, Judy Karrole, and Fr Theodore Pulcini. Finally, I am most grateful to my family, my sons Fr Raphael Daly and John Daly for their very positive criticisms of the work, and to my wife Elfriede Daly who was with me on every page with her encouragement and her special wisdom.

Preface

The purpose of this writing is primarily to offer hope to the many people who find themselves no longer part of the faith community of their childhood. A very large part of those are known as the "inactive Catholics."

There are many reasons why so many have left the Roman Catholic Church. Much has to do with our increasingly secular culture, which has taken over many of our social institutions. But the events over the past half century within the Church itself have caused many to leave. I have entitled this work *The Choice of Orthodoxy* because I believe that, properly understood, Orthodoxy could provide a spiritual home for those seeking the apostolic Church, which dates from the first Pentecost and has retained the fullness of the mystery of the Church.

Many of those who have ceased to be part of the Roman Catholic Church received very little or no instruction in the faith. This lack of knowledge has led to varying degrees of confusion and disbelief. I believe that many have not only not been catechized, they have not even heard the Gospel. Christ and the Church have been presented in American culture with hostility and falsehood. The present confusion is understandable.

Consequently, before speaking about the Orthodox Church, and given the level of agnosticism and atheism in our country, it is necessary to consider first the credibility of Christianity itself. This means the primary question will be the identity of Jesus of Nazareth. He answered that question in the Gospels. How one responds to that identity will determine the course of one's life. Then this inquiry must go beyond His identity to the examination of His life and work. Only then can we understand the importance of the Church that He founded.

We may then raise the questions of the differences between Catholicism and Orthodoxy and how those differences led to changes in the Catholic Church. It is my personal belief that much centers around the issue of Holy Tradition and its importance in the ongoing life of the Church.

I chose to be part of the Orthodox Church more than forty years ago. I have no intention to proselytize. I write out of concern for my own family and the many who have found themselves in a spiritual wasteland. Although my intended readership is primarily "inactive Catholics," what I have written may be helpful to Anglicans and other Protestant people. Christianity was founded in the ancient East. It is still there in its fullness. The Orthodox Church has been in North America for more than two centuries. For those unable to find a home in Western Christianity it is there.

1

Before Vatican II

What Was It like to Someone Who Was Part of It?

Fifty-eight years ago, in 1964 I entered the final years of a Roman Catholic seminary. In those days it was called the Major Seminary. On the evening of that first day something occurred that has remained in my memory. The seminarians gathered in church for Benediction of the Blessed Sacrament. At the end of the service a student arose and announced that the closing hymn would be "Go Tell It on the Mountain." What this Christmas song had to do with the Eucharist, I could not fathom. I would find myself asking that question more than once in my life as a priest.

The fact that I vividly remember that moment tells me that something in my mind suspected problems. I enjoyed my seminary years. I certainly did not become paranoid about what was happening in the Church, but I approached changes in the life of the Church with measured caution. My seminary education was structured around church history in which we studied the life, teachings, and worship of the Church as things developed through the Church Fathers and Councils. It was orthodox. They were good years. The seminary made me a lifelong student.

When I was assigned to my first parish in 1970, the youth choir sang the music of *Jesus Christ Superstar* accompanied by guitars at Mass. The same question arose in my mind: what did this music have to do with the Eucharist? Several of the older and wiser laypeople questioned the appropriateness of this music. The sister who was the director told me that this music was played on Vatican Radio, which apparently justified its use in church. A friend who is now a bishop in the Orthodox Church told me that he knew things were in trouble when his Catholic grade school sang "Jeremiah Was a Bullfrog" at Mass. I was uncomfortable with many of the music choices, but I could not come up with a succinct (theological) reason why this music was out of place. This would come only after I was exposed to Orthodox theology. I will go into that later.

In the year and a half I spent in that parish, I felt the same discomfort with the Archdiocese of Detroit that I felt with the modern music. It seemed to me that the Church was becoming more man-centered and less God-centered. Issues of social justice were paramount. In 1976 the Archdiocese hosted the "Call to Action" convention, which challenged the teachings of the Church on birth control, the ordination of women, and other traditional practices. The participants, although appointed by their bishops, were largely liberal Catholics.

Today, six decades after the Second Vatican Council, the Catholic Church is almost unrecognizable. So many of the changes involved the Eucharist. The parish church was "ground zero" where the changes were experienced by the laity. Politicians use the word "change" almost always in the positive. "We need change." The same spirit was embraced by many in the days after the Council. The "old" needed to be changed. We now live in a time of widespread confusion regarding the most fundamental beliefs and practices of the Catholic Church.

There is no doubt that American Catholicism has changed. As a man in his eighties I remember the pre-Vatican II Church well. It was in that Church that I was formed. The awareness of that Church is quickly passing away. People under the age of sixty have little or no memory of it. Those who do are now aging senior citizens. For the sake of the younger group, I will share some memories of what it was like. Here I speak from my own personal experience.

The Church of My Childhood

I was born in 1938. I attended the local parish school in the 1940s and early 1950s. The parish that I attended was in a small town outside Detroit. In its early years the school had only four classrooms. The students were taught by Franciscan sisters. Despite the small size of our parish, we were made aware of a world that went beyond our small town, and of a Church that went beyond the parish. We belonged to an arch-diocese with a cardinal at its head. We never saw him, nor did we see the pope in Rome, but we were part of something that went far beyond our little parish. And, most important, this made us aware of the world of the Kingdom of God, which made us a part of a transcendent world beyond ourselves. The sisters in their habits were a very real sign of the presence in this world of the life in the future Kingdom. Those who lived in those years will remember greeting a sister or priest who entered the classroom with "Good morning, Sister" or

"Good morning, Father." This was the value of the parochial education. It revealed to us one of the most important things in the world, our identity. Secular education never opens the door to heavenly realities. Man is left to find an identity in an enclosed earthly existence.

In the 1950s Will Herberg wrote his bestselling book, *Protestant, Catholic and Jew.* Among the many points he made, Herberg discerned that America was not one great melting pot, but three. People identified themselves as either Protestant, Catholic, or Jew. Americans found their identity in their religious faith. Today that is no longer true. Our present culture is obsessed with identity. The secular world cannot answer that fundamental question.

Religious education of the parochial school was fundamental to the programs of the parochial school. It was certainly not a matter of learning "Catholic mathematics" or anything of that sort. It was far more fundamental. It had to do with our identity as human beings. The most basic of human questions were asked on the first page of the *Baltimore Catechism Number One.* "Who made me?" The answer was "God made me." "Why did God make me?" "He made me to know Him, love Him, and serve Him in this world and to be happy with Him forever in heaven." The most important questions of human existence were addressed to children at the age of six or seven. Even at a young age we understood what those words meant.

Our small church had its own sense of holiness. The statues of Christ and His mother made us aware that, although unseen, they were present in our church life. We assembled in church each morning prior to going over to the school for classes. The Mass was a holy mystery that I could not completely understand. But it was something that took us into the heavenly world amidst the sound of banging lunch boxes as the children entered the church.

One moment remains strong in my memory. It occurred at what was called the "Forty Hours Devotion." These were several days of eucharistic devotion by the entire parish which ended with Benediction and a procession with the Blessed Sacrament. I remember being dressed in a red cassock with a lace surplice and carrying a lighted taper in the procession. We sang *"Pange Lingua Gloriosi"* [Sing, (My) Tongue, the (Savior's) Glory]. The priests of the neighboring parishes chanted the Litany of the Saints in Latin with the response *"Ora pro nobis"* [Pray for us]. (My County Cork Irish father liked that part the best as he joined in singing "Oh Rop row Nobus" with an Irish brogue.) That service was an experience of something numinous and transcendent. It had everything to do with the Eucharist.

Whether that world still exists in some Catholic parish I do not know. In those days seventy percent of Catholics attended Sunday Mass. I do not believe that the kind of parish I grew up in can ever return. It was a world of common faith centered on the parish.

The Changes

As I began my life as a priest, the Mass was already in English. How did music like *Jesus Christ Superstar* find its way into the Mass? We might say by default. There were few Catholic hymns in English. Most were Marian hymns such as "On this day, O beautiful Mother" or "Daily, daily sing to Mary." Following the Second Vatican Council, the obvious sources were Protestant hymns with mixed results. Prior to Vatican II, the old missal contained the words for specific musical texts. Old Catholics will remember these as the "Introit," "Gradual," "Offertory Verse," and "Communion Antiphon."

Prior to Vatican II, the Missal contained all the parts for the Mass. It contained the priest's prayers, the readings from Scripture, and as noted, the musical texts for the Mass. In the years after Vatican II, the Missal was broken up in a process that took several years. The priest's parts were now in a new book called the *Sacramentary*. The epistles and Gospels were contained in the book called the *Lectionary*. But a book for the musical texts of the Mass was left unpublished. That opened the door to all sorts of music that had little to do with the Mass. The freedom to choose music for each service opened the door to other "freedoms." I remember Fr Aidan Cavanaugh, our professor of Liturgy, telling us not to "tinker with the liturgy." Unfortunately, there was a lot of tinkering.

In the year after my ordination, I had the opportunity to travel in Europe. It was in Holland that I witnessed a celebration of the Eucharist that left me speechless. It was held in an outdoor camp. A Dutch priest sat at a card table, with the chalice and paten in front of him. He was dressed in a suit and tie. Papers were passed out and the people began to sing "Joshua Fought the Battle of Jericho" in Dutch! To this day I cannot find words to express my reaction to that music. Nothing against the Dutch, but this left me speechless. I questioned what this priest thought he was doing. It appeared more as a picnic than the sacrifice of the Mass.

In the years following the Vatican Council many of the churches were "renovated." The high altars were removed.

Table altars took center place. Communion rails and side altars were taken away. Statues were removed. People stood to receive Communion. Communion was given in the hand.

The rite itself was changed. Many took liberties that had nothing to do with the teaching of Vatican II. Through the internet I have seen videos of the "Clown Mass," the "Polka Mass," and the "Pride Mass." Liturgical committees imposed certain themes on the Mass, overlooking the fact that the Mass has its own unchanged theme, the mystical sacrifice of the Son of God.

The Orthodox theologian, Fr John Meyendorff, stated in a class I attended, "The Liturgy is either *eschatological* (meaning it is in direct contact with heavenly Kingdom) or it is *theater*. It is not theater!" he said emphatically. He made a very important point. In many instances, the more extreme Masses have moved from worship into theater—and actually, rather bad theater. The congregation becomes simply an audience to what is going on. I don't believe that the bishops of Vatican II ever intended this outcome.

Today some Catholics, mostly older ones, have continued to attend the parish using the *Novus Ordo* or post-Vatican II liturgy. Others have found churches where the pre-Vatican II Mass is still celebrated in Latin, and others, many others, have ceased to attend church. Why have so many stopped attending Sunday Mass? There is no one reason. It is likely to do with the personal experience of each individual. But collectively it has been widespread. What caused this loss?

The Changing Culture

Some would argue that the loss of active church members was caused by the secularized culture of the nation. The Church does not exist apart from the surrounding culture. That will always be the case. Has the changing American culture been influential in the changes of the Church? I think the answer is that it has. But that is not the whole answer.

The founding of our country coincides almost exactly with the first of a series of "revolutions." The first was the Industrial Revolution, beginning about 1760. Then came the French, the Darwinian, the Freudian, the Marxist, the Civil Rights, the Sexual, the Feminist, and what might be called the "Gender Revolution." Each of these revolutions brought about changes for the individual, the family, and the nation. In the 1960s the "pot boiled over." As Bob Dylan wrote, "The Times, They Are A-changin'." He was right; they were.

Of extreme importance is the fact that the sixties was the decade of the Second Vatican Council, and its consequences changed the Catholic Church in unexpected ways. The Church was changing in a whirlwind of cultural changes. Several of these revolutions contained a decidedly anti-Christian viewpoint, e.g., the French Revolution, the Sexual Revolution, and the Marxist Revolution. Some changes were beneficial. Certainly the changes in health care, food production, and transportation were very beneficial, but the secularization of the culture was not.

The thoughts of Karl Marx (1818–1883) and Friedrich Nietzsche (1844–1900) have given rise to the secular view of reality widely accepted by the world of academia. Marx has also given the world its almost complete focus on economic issues above all other considerations. We have become the world's greatest consumers.

In the most important discussions of social issues, secular society has set its own limitations to the discourse. Religion does not have a seat at the table. This has been especially true in questions of human sexuality, despite the strongly held view of religious people. Individual human "rights" take precedence above all other considerations.

Christianity and Catholicism in particular are under siege in our country. Churches are burned, statues and religious images are defaced with diabolic signs. The secularists in our Congress were horrified that a serious Catholic judge was appointed to the Supreme Court. They simply could not comprehend that someone would be guided in their moral choices by something other than personal views or some flavor of secular morality.

One landmark of secularism was the *Roe versus Wade* decision of the Supreme Court, which created a constitutionally protected right to abortion. After a half century of this decision more than sixty million lives have been terminated. That is approximately the population of Italy. The death of six million Jews was a horrible act of genocide, but who speaks up for these lost Americans? Even with the recent Supreme Court decision overturning *Roe versus Wade*, the war for the unborn continues.

There is nothing new in anti-Catholicism. It was present in colonial Maryland. In the mid-1800s German, Irish, and other Catholic immigrants were a challenge to Protestantism. Those looking for employment would find the local paper stating firmly "No Irish Need Apply." This anti-Catholic hostility gave rise to the attacks on persons and churches in the years of the Nativist and Know-Nothing uprisings. The growth of Catholicism was considered a threat to the nation. Bishop Francis Kenrick of Philadelphia (1796–1863), who was both a scholar and educator, led the Catholic Church in the midst of the burning of churches, convents, and homes. He had asked if the Catholic children attending public schools might read from the Catholic Douay version of the Bible. This was seen as a threat to everything American by the adversaries of the Catholic Church.

In present day America, one thing remains unchanged; the only acceptable form of bigotry in American academia is anti-Catholicism. When John Kennedy ran for president, many feared that he would take orders from the pope. But despite the external hostility of those decades, the Church did not suffer the loss of its members. It grew in numbers.

One might hope that in the face of the current secularist hostility, the Catholic Church might marshal its forces as it did in the days of the "Know-Nothings." After the riots, Bishop Kenrick ended his efforts to influence the public education system and began encouraging the creation of Catholic schools, with seventeen being founded by 1860. Today, the Catholic schools as well as parish churches are closing.

The secular education of children has had a very negative effect on the religious life of our nation. Today the forces of secularism have had a disastrous effect on our country. I fear for the children. At very young ages they are exposed to the most extreme social theories regarding their race. Some in the medical world believe that it is perfectly appropriate for children to change their "gender." Christian parents are finding themselves in a world that is not unlike the totalitarian regimes of the twentieth century.

All Christian groups, including the Orthodox Churches, have been affected by secularism. Many young people are lost to the Church during their college years. Young Orthodox Christians are not immune to the forces of secularism. We too lose many in the college years.

Although the secular world has very serious effects on the life of Catholic people, we cannot completely blame secular society for the condition of the American Catholic Church. The problems lie within. I believe that one of the major causes is the disregard of Holy Tradition by the leaders of the Catholic Church.

2

What Went Wrong?

What Was Lost Amidst the Changes?

How Important Is Holy Tradition?

The battle cry of the Protestant Reformation was *Sola Scriptura,* i.e., only the Bible. What was rejected was Tradition. The Catholic Church insisted that Divine Truth came through both Scripture and Tradition. Tradition in this sense is not simply human customs, or the *tradition of men* (Colossians 2.8), but what St Paul spoke of: *Keep the traditions just as I delivered them to you* (1 Corinthians 11.2).

The Second Vatican Council's Dogmatic Constitution on Divine Revelation, *Dei Verbum,* explains the relationship between Tradition and Scripture: "There exists a close connection and communication between sacred Tradition and sacred Scripture. For both of them, flowing from the same divine wellspring, in a certain way merge into a unity and tend toward the same end" (*Dei Verbum* 2.9).

"Therefore the Apostles, handing on what they themselves had received, warn the faithful to hold fast to the traditions which they have learned either by word of mouth or by letter (see 2 Thessalonians 2.15), and to fight in defense of the faith handed on to them once for all (see Jude 1.3–4.). Now what was handed on by the Apostles includes everything which contributes toward the holiness of life and increases in faith of the peoples of God; and so the Church, in her teaching, life and worship, perpetuates and hands on to all generations all that she herself is, all that she believes" (*Dei Verbum* 2.8).

"The words of the holy fathers witness to the presence of this living tradition, whose wealth is poured into the practice and life of the believing and praying Church." The Council affirmed the importance of Tradition. "Scripture and Tradition must be accepted and honored with equal feeling of devotion and reverence" (*Dei Verbum* 2.9).

Its affirmation of the importance of Tradition was later repeated by the *Catholic Catechism*. Through Tradition, "the Church, in her doctrine, life and worship, perpetuates and transmits to every generation all that she herself is, all that she believes. The sayings of the holy Fathers are a witness to the life-giving presence of this Tradition, showing how its riches are poured out in the practice and life of the Church, in her belief and her prayer" (*Catechism of the Catholic Church*, Article 2.78).

Was Tradition "accepted and honored with equal feeling of devotion and reverence"? I would answer, not entirely. The Catholic Church possessed and officially honored Holy Tradition, but in practice in the days following Vatican II, it was not seen as the ground of continuity and change.

It is unfortunate that Vatican II did not itemize the elements of Holy Tradition. Rev. John Hardon, S.J., in his book, *The Catholic Catechism*, gives a clearer understanding of Holy Tradition: "There are instruments or channels by which Tradition has been and is now transmitted to the people of God: professions of faith, the Church's liturgy, unvarying practices from apostolic times, writings of the Church Fathers, even archeological monuments."[1]

---

[1] John A. Hardon, S.J., *The Catholic Catechism; A Contemporary Catechism of the Teachings of the Catholic Church* (New York: Image, 1975), 48.

What greater guide could the Church use for change than the two thousand years of experience we call the Holy Tradition? The promised Holy Spirit has guided the Church in all truth.

When changes were implemented in the American parishes, I never heard or saw any reference to the importance of Tradition. It seemed rather that Tradition belonged to the dogmatic life of the Church, to its apologetics, not to all other aspects of church life. Many found the changes disturbing, but the encouragement of the bishops and the authority of the local pastor rendered the faithful powerless to do anything. In the early days of liturgical change one layman who used his Latin and English missal to follow the Mass asked me, "Why are they changing the Mass? I have been able to participate by praying along with the priest. I can no longer do this. I am now a spectator." For many the Mass was no longer a time of prayer.

Holy Tradition in Orthodoxy

When our Lord was on this earth, He made three specific promises to the Apostles regarding the Holy Spirit. The Father would send the Holy Spirit. The Spirit would lead them in all truth. And the Holy Spirit would be with them forever. These texts may be found in the Gospel according to St John (14.12–25 and 16.12–25). Both the Catholic and the Orthodox Churches believe that the Holy Spirit did not leave the Church when the Bible was written. Both see the Holy Spirit as the source of Scripture and Tradition.

Fr Thomas Hopko provides a clear understanding of Holy Tradition in the Orthodox Church:

The ongoing life of God's people is called Holy Tradition. . . . The Gospel and the other writings of the Apostolic Church form the heart of the Christian Tradition and inspiration of all that developed in later ages . . . although containing many written documents, Holy Tradition is not merely a body of literature. It is, on the contrary, the total life and experience of the entire Church transferred from place to place and from generation to generation. . . . Among the elements that make up the Holy Tradition of the Church, the Bible holds first place. Next comes the Church's liturgical life and its prayer, then its dogmatic decisions and the acts of the approved councils, the writings of the Church Fathers, the lives of the saints, the canon laws, and finally the iconographic tradition together with other inspired forms of creative artistic expressions such as music and architecture. All of the elements of Holy Tradition are organically linked together in real life. None of them stands alone. None may be separated or isolated from the other or from the wholeness of the life of the Church. All come alive in the actual living of the life of the Church in every age and generation.[2]

The Elements of Holy Tradition

This chart illustrates, albeit inadequately, how the Father has revealed Himself in and through the Son. The Son is Truth. This revelation is made available through the Holy Spirit in the life of the Church. Somewhat as in a mirror, each element of Holy Tradition contains and reflects the One Truth. As the lines indicate, each element of Holy Tradition must be in harmony with the others. What is expressed in the Creed and liturgical prayers of the Church must be the same truth that is contained in the icons and spoken of by the Fathers of the Church.

[2] Thomas Hopko, *The Orthodox Faith*, vol. 1: *Doctrine & Scripture*, 2nd ed. (Yonkers, NY: St Vladimir's Seminary Press, 2016), 22.

HOLY TRADITION

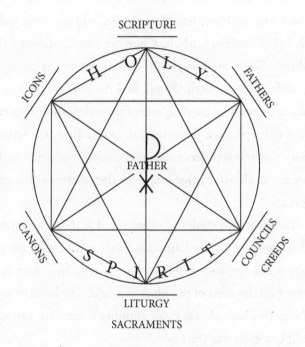

SCRIPTURE

H O L Y

ICONS

FATHERS

FATHER

CANONS

COUNCILS
CREEDS

S P I R I T

LITURGY
SACRAMENTS

It is my belief that many of the problems arising from the changes in the life of the Catholic Church are a result of having a limited understanding of the full extent and importance of Holy Tradition. Orthodoxy, as noted above, regards the art, the architecture, and the music of the Church as integral parts of Holy Tradition along with the Creed, the Councils, and the Church Fathers.

Architecturally, the traditional form of the church was a three-part building (sanctuary, nave, and narthex) facing east. Many modern Catholic Churches have abandoned that tradition. Some are completely unrecognizable as churches. The differences between the old and the new church can be best experienced by entering one of the older ethnic churches in the older parts of the American cities. They still retain a beauty and transcendence that one cannot experience in the more recent churches. One prays that they survive in the coming years.

The great cathedrals of Europe stand as the greatest physical testimonies of the Christian Faith of countless people. Many are more than a thousand years old. They were built without all the tools of the modern world. The builders lived in homes without electricity or running water. One can only say, "How great was their faith!"

Church Music Must Be Orthodox

The music of the Church is part of the wholeness of the life of the Church. It must express the same Truth that is revealed in the Scripture, confessed in the Creed, depicted in the icons, and professed by the Church Fathers. *Jesus Christ Superstar* fails on all counts. It is not an expression of the Faith of the Church. In other words, it is not orthodox!

The art of the Orthodox Church is its icons. What is depicted in the icon must be in accord with the Holy Tradition. In Western art, human models were used for paintings of Christ and the Virgin Mary. This is not allowed in Orthodox icons. These icons are based on the more ancient icons of the Church. They are the art of the Church and not the art of the artist. The same is true of the music and prayers of the Church. They too must express the same Truth as found in the New Testament. In summary, each element of Holy Tradition must be orthodox.

In the Orthodox Church this understanding is simply a given. No priest or bishop would begin a program of change or renovation without reference to the Holy Tradition in all aspects of the life of the Church.

What has happened in some parishes might almost be a recurrence of the eighth-century movement called Iconoclasm. With the authority of the Byzantine Emperor, religious art was outlawed. This eventually led to the Seventh Ecumenical Council, which defended the use of the icons in Church.

This council is accepted by both the Orthodox and the Catholic Church.

Sadly the renovation of many churches involved the
removal of much of their art. In my home parish there was a
statue of the Blessed Virgin. It was a very beautiful statue. To
me as a child, in some way I cannot explain, that was Mary,
the Mother of Christ. The last time I saw the statue, it was in
what had been a confessional, off to the side. No matter how
I felt about other churches being renovated, this was different.
This was my church. I did not like what I saw. This gave me a
completely different appreciation of how countless people felt
about what happened in their parish churches. So much faith
had involved the art of the Church.

Several years ago a young Orthodox man told me something that he experienced in his senior trip. Although Orthodox, he attended a Protestant Christian high school. The trip
was to Cappadocia in modern-day Turkey. Upon entering one
of the caves, the young people were shocked at the presence of
Byzantine icons on the ancient walls. "Where are these from?
What are they?" The young man answered, "They are icons.
They look exactly like my home church back in America."

The importance of Holy Tradition was not part of my
seminary education, and I am convinced that it was not part

of the education of the men who became the bishops of the post-Vatican II Church.

The disregard for the importance of Holy Tradition in the life of the modern Catholic Church is, I believe, the root cause of the chaotic changes that occurred in the years after the Council. The words of the bishops of Vatican II, "Scripture and Tradition must be accepted and honored with equal feeling of devotion and reverence"—these words went unheard, or unheeded.

Some years ago, one of the meetings of the National Catholic Bishops Conference was televised. One of the bishops arose and with anxiety in his voice said, "We do not know what to tell the people about building a new Church. We have no guidelines. How are we to guide the people when we do not know?" This was a very revealing remark.

Are There Two Different Traditions?

Although Orthodoxy and Catholicism understand Tradition to be vital in the life of the Church, they differ in two regards. As noted, Orthodoxy is more explicit in the various elements of Tradition—namely, art and architecture. Secondly, in Orthodoxy, Tradition carries more authority in the ongoing life of the Church. Serious changes are never made without reference to the Holy Tradition. Both Churches affirm the importance of Tradition. The difference lies not in theory but in practice. Did the Catholic Church somehow forget the importance of Tradition? Certainly not in theory, but it did in the living-out-of-church practice on the level of the diocese and parish.

The difference between the practice of the two Churches lies in the exercise of authority. The more decentralized the authority in the Church, as is the situation in the Orthodox Church, the greater is the importance given to Holy Tradition. The more *centralized* the authority, as is the case in the Catholic Church, the less is the importance given to Holy Tradition. Over the centuries authority in the Western Church became more and more centralized in the Roman papacy. Over time Tradition ended up on the "back burner" as the papacy rose in authority.

The Catholic position on the status of the pope was dogmatically defined at the First Vatican Council of 1869–1870 in the document *Pastor aeternus*. This document affirmed the pope's judicial supremacy, insisting that there is "no higher authority," not even an ecumenical council, to which appeal can be made from a papal judgment. It also dogmatically defined the infallibility of the pope. This council was held under the authority of Pope Pius IX, who reigned from 1846 to 1878. These two declarations gave the pope immense power over the Catholic Church. Historians may view the First Vatican Council as of greater influence on the life of the Catholic Church than the Second Vatican Council. Vatican I made the pope a virtual autocrat.

Pope Pius IX is said to have remarked to a cardinal who evidently raised the issue of Tradition, "*Tradition? I am Tradition.*" If that is true, then the phrase "*Roma locuta, causa finita*" [Rome has spoken, the case is closed] became the rule of the day. One need look no further for permission to do something. The important question was "What does Rome say?" As long as everyone lived by that rule, things could not get out of hand. On the other hand, if one did not uphold that authority, then "anything goes." And as some might say, everything went!

I believe that we have arrived at that point in the Church in Germany. Things have reached a point where some priests not only disregard Tradition, but even state that St Paul was simply wrong! If the German Church goes into schism, what authority will guide them in their beliefs and practices? Bible? Tradition? Papacy? Themselves?

Over the past fifty years the importance of Tradition has been lost throughout large parts of the Catholic Church. Today one senses what amounts to hostility toward Tradition.

Issues beyond Tradition

In the present American Catholic Church the bishops do not speak with one voice. They are indecisive on a number of issues. Some are very permissive to those priests who act in very untraditional ways, and very critical of conservative priests who wish to retain the old Latin-Rite Mass. The sexual scandals associated with the clergy have caused many to leave the Catholic Church, both in North America and in Europe. Those scandals have been tragic for all involved. Back in the 1960s one heard rumors, but I was not really aware of the magnitude of the problem.

In the 1970s and the 1980s thousands of priests left the priesthood. Why? Again, I can only offer my own opinion. In those decades the church became very "man-centered." If the priest saw his vocation as simply one path among others to serve mankind, he might well begin to question the value of what he was doing. Others were doing so much more for suffering humanity. If his vocation was not supernatural, he would ask why he was doing these things and living under enforced celibacy.

How often did we hear, "But the Mass is a meal!" The understanding of the Mass as a sacrifice was losing its importance. Both the priesthood and the Eucharist were being undermined. In his own parish any man or woman could distribute Holy Communion, so what was the big deal? I think the same may be said for the religious [that is, monastics]. One need not lead a consecrated life to minister to human needs. A man-centered church loses its supernatural orientation. The Church was founded to bring human beings into the life of God. The Church is a sacramental reality. It is not simply an institution of social justice.

In the early 1970s I spoke to the old retired pastor of my home parish. He was troubled by the changing Catholic Church. "Being a priest doesn't mean anything anymore." I believe he expressed the feelings of many priests. The pastor of the church I was serving at that time, when becoming aware of all that was going on, said, "Do they think the Church was just started yesterday?" His question was very insightful.

The reasons why the American Catholic Church lost millions of members certainly go beyond what I have said here. Those of the older generation no longer felt they were in the same Catholic Church. Those who grew up in the post-Vatican II Church often found the new liturgy uninspiring. Others left because of the scandals and the reaction of the bishops to those scandals. *Many have never been adequately catechized,* and this is one of the major reasons for the departure of so many. Today many are agnostic or atheists. The fact remains—many have become inactive or have completely left the Church.

The sad truth is that millions have ceased to attend Mass. They have ceased to worship. This has to do with more than simply being an active Christian. It has to do with who we are as persons. The late Orthodox theologian Fr Alexander Schmemann insisted that human identity was not simply being *homo sapiens,* but rather *homo adorans*, man the worshipper. Secular man has lost something essential to his very being. The years following Vatican II were a time when many Catholic people ceased to worship. What was lost was the central place of Christ in our life and in our worship. Perhaps the move of the tabernacle to someplace off to the side was symbolic of the decentralization of Christ Himself. Holy images were removed from the churches. There was little difference between a Catholic church and a Protestant church. The focus was now on man, civil rights, justice, and peace. These are worthwhile concerns, but the Catholic Church became more man-centered than God-centered. Worship became preoccupied with what *we* were doing, bringing worship in tune with modern culture. We ceased looking beyond the altar table into the Kingdom of God. The priest was now looking at us. We were certainly not worshiping as ancient Christians did. Here I offer an example of the ancient spirit of divine worship. When we compare today's liturgical language with the most ancient liturgy of the Church, that of St James of Jerusalem, there is a striking difference.

> O SOVEREIGN Lord our God, condemn me not, defiled with a multitude of sins: for, behold, I have come to this Thy divine and heavenly mystery, not as being worthy; but looking only to Thy goodness, I direct my voice to Thee: God be merciful to me, a sinner; I have sinned against Heaven, and before Thee, and am unworthy to come into the presence of this Thy holy and spiritual table, upon which Thy only-begotten Son, and our Lord Jesus Christ, is mystically set forth as a sacrifice for me, a sinner, and stained with every spot. Wherefore I present to Thee this supplication and thanksgiving, that Thy Spirit the Comforter may be sent down upon

me, strengthening and fitting me for this service; and count me worthy to make known without condemnation the word, delivered from Thee by me to the people, in Christ Jesus our Lord, with whom Thou art blessed, together with Thine all-holy, and good, and live-giving, and consubstantial Spirit, now and ever, and to all eternity. Amen.[3]

What a contrast! This prayer expresses the belief that the priest and the people now are approaching the presence of the All-Holy God. Here we find the sense of holy mystery that we so long for. This is God-centered worship. This worship stands in strong contrast with the liturgical efforts of the 1970s to "make it relevant." *Kumbaya* would be totally out of place here. For many this was the loss not only of beautiful worship, but also of Christ Himself.

Of course Christ was not totally lost, but His place was out of focus. Human beings need something more than a liturgy that makes them feel good. They need worship that brings them into a transcendent relationship with God. To

---

[3] *The Divine Liturgy of James the Holy Apostle and Brother of the Lord*, in The Ante-Nicene Fathers, vol. 7 (Buffalo: The Christian Literature Company, 1886), 537–550, at 537.

lose the centrality of Christ means the loss of our identity with Him, of what made us one with Him and the Holy Trinity. Without this what is the point of going to Mass?

I believe that Orthodoxy offers hope to many of those who find themselves no longer able to be part of any church in any real way. *But before examining Orthodoxy, the very credibility of Christianity itself must be examined.* There is much more to the problem than simply how one feels about the Church. It is a matter of belief or unbelief.

What is the foundation of the Christian Faith? How credible is Christianity? Is there something in Christianity more than simply a moral code to live by? What is meant by salvation? *To address these questions one must begin with the identity of Jesus of Nazareth. That is the paramount issue, and the most important question of all.*

One may ask, "Is this really necessary? Can we not take the identity of Jesus for granted? Do not most Christians have a clear understanding of who He is, why He came to the world, and what He has done for mankind? Does not even the most inactive Catholic know that He is God?" I don't think so. God only knows what they believe. Where would they learn the truth about our Lord? The un-churched are without question the un-catechized and even the un-evangelized. If one's parents stopped going to church, the children's awareness of Christ does not get beyond the Christmas tree and the Easter eggs. Some churches present Jesus as a really nice guy who loves everybody and tolerates every form of sin. Religion on TV often presents Jesus as a successful financial planner who came to make us rich. Reading the obituaries in most papers would lead one to believe that everybody goes to heaven. As a consequence of this widespread ignorance, nothing can be taken for granted. We cannot talk about Jesus, the mystery of salvation, or the Church unless we speak about the Jesus of the Gospels and the Faith "once delivered to the saints." It is imperative that we begin here.

I will not begin by raising the question regarding the existence or non-existence of God. This was the approach of St Thomas Aquinas. I do not question the value of his theology, but at this time in history I do not think it is the best way to begin the defense of Christianity. Non-Christian religions also "believe in God." Proof for the existence of God is more an issue to be debated by philosophy than by theology. Christianity is not based on a book, but on historical events. The fundamental event of the Christian Faith is the Incarnation of the Son of God, Jesus Christ. It is with Him, His identity, and His credibility, that we must begin.

3

Jesus of Nazareth

Who Do You Say that He Is?

Was Jesus Christ Truly Human?

The Church regards Jesus as True God and True Man. We know that He was a first century Jew. As a child He underwent what was common to Jewish boys: he was circumcised, he was taken to the Temple, and he attended the synagogue. Sometime around the age of thirty he began a public ministry proclaiming repentance and the imminence of the Kingdom of God. His miracles of healing drew large crowds of followers.

After about three years He was crucified by the Roman authorities at the instigation of the religious leaders of the time. And by the testimony of His disciples, He arose from the dead on the third day. The basic facts of His life are recorded in the four Gospels.

What kind of person was He? He could be compassionate to the sinner, but extremely harsh on the Pharisees. Very revealing however, was His treatment of the powerless. In His treatment of women and children Jesus reveals how He valued individual persons. He broke what was considered normal social behavior. He talked to women. Jewish men did not speak to women they did not know.

As Jesus went about his public ministry, He was accompanied by a number of women who provided for Him. They were with Him at His death and were the first to hear of His Resurrection. St John tells us in his Gospel that when Jesus was thirsty, he approached a Samaritan woman at Jacob's Well. He asked for a drink of water. The woman was shocked that He would speak to her—a *woman* and a Samaritan. Even more surprising is that He would tell this non-Jewish woman that He was in fact the Messiah! Martha and Mary of Bethany were close personal friends of Jesus. He came back to Bethany to visit them after the death of their brother Lazarus. The woman caught in adultery was saved by Jesus from those who would stone her to death. Jesus was the best friend that women have ever had. Jesus did not simply debate the Mosaic

Law with a group of learned men in the temple or synagogue; He spent His time with men, women, and children.

In the Roman Empire, which permitted parents to sell or even kill their children, the behavior of Jesus toward children is striking. One example of His interaction with children revealed how He regarded them.

> Then they also brought infants to Him that He might touch them; but when the disciples saw it, they rebuked them. But Jesus called them to Him and said, "Let the little children come to Me, and do not forbid them; for of such is the kingdom of God. Assuredly, I say to you, whoever does not receive the kingdom of God as a little child will by no means enter it." (Luke 18.15–17)

> At that time the disciples came to Jesus, saying, "Who then is greatest in the kingdom of heaven?" Then Jesus called a little child to Him, set him in the midst of them, and said, "Assuredly, I say to you, unless you are converted and become as little children, you will by no means enter the kingdom of heaven. Therefore whoever humbles himself as this little child is the greatest in the kingdom of heaven. Whoever receives one little child like this in My name receives Me. Whoever causes one

of these little ones who believe in Me to sin, it would be better for him if a millstone were hung around his neck, and he were drowned in the depth of the sea." (Matthew 18.1–6)

Under the first Christian Emperor, Constantine, children could no longer be sold or killed.

What Was the Message of Jesus?

During his ministry Jesus taught many things, but the very first words He spoke are most important. *Repent, for the Kingdom of Heaven is at hand* (Matthew 4.17). What did he mean by these words? In common usage *repent* means to express sorrow for past deeds. I was curious about the word *repent*. From what language did it come into English? Its root in Latin means "to creep" along the ground. I was not completely satisfied with what I found, but I did learn one fascinating thing. The internet site that I used showed a graph illustrating how often any given word has been used over the past several hundred years. What is said about the use of the word *repent* is very interesting. Back in 1850 the word was widely used. Today it has almost disappeared from our language. It seems that the world of 1850 was more concerned with the business of repenting than is our present time.

The original Greek word in the New Testament for repentance is *metanoia*. This word is not about regret and handwringing. *Meta* indicates *change*. *Nous* in Greek means the *mind*. Metanoia means more than regret; it means a change of the mind, not a change of opinion. Again, it is the mind itself that needs to change, not just its opinions. Repentance means to look at things differently. In His later teaching Jesus would ask His hearers to "change their mind" especially in their understanding of the Jewish Law or Torah. This was the content of His famous Sermon on the Mount. The call to change our minds is as true today as it was then. A Christian cannot look at reality from a strictly secular perspective. With understanding it is imperative that we change our moral life.

The second word used by Jesus in His opening sermon was the word "kingdom." Jesus now announced that the Kingdom of God was at hand. This was something new. It came with Him. It was a statement of the sovereignty of God over the world and in the world. This went beyond just a claim of authority; it was a living and active presence of God. The Kingdom of God is something in the world and, as He said to Pilate, a kingdom "not of this world." It was present and yet to come. It was an absolute claim of authority in the world. Although a Christian is called to render to Caesar the things that are Caesar's, he cannot live with divided loyalties. That is the problem for those who try to live in harmony with the secular world. That is the quandary of the American Catholic bishops.

The New Commandment

Of all things that Jesus taught, the commandment of love is central. When Jesus announced that He would come again and judge the world, the basis of that judgement would be how human beings treated one another. Whatever one did or failed to do to the least of His brethren, Jesus said they were doing or failing to do to Him. Jesus did not reject the Law, but the ultimate criteria for Christian morality was—and still is—love or charity. Jesus went beyond the Old Testament law of loving the Lord and loving one's neighbor as oneself. He went beyond those two traditional laws and stated that we were to love one another *as He loved us*. And He gave His life for the world. Love is not the antithesis of hatred, but of selfishness. One might conclude that a lifetime of choosing oneself could lead to an eternity of one's own company.

St John would teach that God *is* Love. That being true, there is no way of spending eternity with this Self-giving God if we have spent a lifetime making the choice of ourselves. Spending eternity in solitary confinement is a grim thought.

Is Jesus Truly Divine?

Jesus most certainly regarded the question of His identity as very important. He wanted to know who people thought He was. He pointedly asked His apostles where they stood on the question. The conversation regarding His identity took place near the town of Caesarea Philippi. The events of that day were recorded by three of the four Evangelists, Matthew, Mark, and Luke. Given the fact that Matthew was very likely present, I will quote only his narrative.

When Jesus came into the region of Caesarea Philippi, He asked His disciples, saying, "Who do men say that I, the Son of Man, am?'" So they said, "Some say John the Baptist, some Elijah, and others Jeremiah or one of the prophets." He said to them, "But who do you say that I am?" Simon Peter answered and said, "You are the Christ, the Son of the living God." Jesus answered and said to him, "Blessed are you, Simon Bar-Jonah, for flesh and blood has not revealed this to you, but My Father who is in heaven. And I also say to you that you are Peter, and on this rock I will build My church, and the gates of Hades shall not prevail against it. And I will give you the keys of the kingdom of heaven, and whatever you bind on earth will be bound in heaven, and whatever you loose on earth will be loosed in heaven." Then He commanded His disciples that they should tell no one that He was Jesus the Christ. (Matthew 16.13–20)

The response of Jesus to Peter contains several very important matters. The identity of Jesus was of interest to people. They thought He might be one of the ancient prophets. When asked, Peter confessed Jesus to be the Christ, the Son of the living God. Jesus tells Peter that "flesh and blood did not reveal this to you." Peter's act of faith was assisted by the Father.

Secondly, Jesus spoke of the Father as "My" Father. Here He reveals that He has a special relationship with the Father. It is uniquely personal with Jesus. Peter responds to the question of Jesus by saying, "You are the Christ, the Son of the living God." Jesus accepts the confession of Peter and thereby affirms that He is the Christ, the Son of the Living God.

Jesus then tells Peter, "You are Peter and on this rock I will build My church." Peter's name in Greek is *Petros,* which means "rock." What rock is Jesus referring to? Is it Peter or is it the confession of faith that Peter just made? Peter was the first human being in history who publicly confessed Jesus as Messiah and Son of God. This statement of faith, this confession, is also the rock that is the foundation of the faith of the Church. So was Peter himself the rock, or was the "rock" his confession? I believe that both were intended. Peter's faith and the faith of every Christian is not a matter of opinion. It is an act of trust.

Finally, Jesus spoke of building a Church against which the gates of Hell would not prevail. Jesus did not found a movement; He founded the Church. Lastly Jesus commanded His disciples that "they tell no one that He was Jesus the Christ." His identity was to remain a secret—for the time being.

The question asked by Jesus is a question that is asked of us. Who do *we* say that He is? The consequences are obviously very important. In the process of answering that question, we must consider who Jesus Himself said He was. We know what the Apostles and Evangelists would say when the Gospels were written several decades later, but our consideration of Jesus Christ should also be based on what Jesus said about Himself and the claims He made.

Did Jesus ever say that He was in fact the Messiah? He did, but in a surprising situation. As noted above, Jesus was going through the territory of the Samaritans, a people whom the Jews regarded as only half-Jewish. They worshipped God on Mount Gerizim. Jesus became thirsty. He came upon Jacob's Well. A Samaritan woman was drawing water. Jesus asked her for a drink. She was very much surprised. She was a woman. And she was a Samaritan. In the ensuing conversation Jesus reveals that He knows of her past life and many marriages. The conversation begins to touch on the differences between the Samaritans and the Jews. *Then the woman said to Him, "I know that the Messiah is coming" (who is called Christ). "When He comes, He will tell us all things." Jesus said to her, "I who speak to you am He* (John 4.26). In His statement to this woman, Jesus leaves no doubt about His claim to be the Messiah.

Did Jesus personally say that He was the Son of God? In the ninth chapter of St John's Gospel we are told of an event where Jesus restores the sight of a man born blind. This event troubles the Pharisees. It was done on the Sabbath. Jesus was already a controversial person with the Pharisees. They begin to interrogate the man, then his parents, and then the man again. They end up rejecting both the man and his testimony about Jesus. At that point Jesus looks for the man and has a very revealing conversation with him.

Jesus heard that they had cast him out; and when He had found him, He said to him, "Do you believe in the Son of God?" He answered and said, "Who is He, Lord, that I may believe in Him?" And Jesus said to him, "You have both seen Him and it is He who is talking with you" (John 9.37). Jesus very clearly claims to be the Son of God. Not *a* Son of God but *the* Son of God.

Rejection in Nazareth

Some of Jesus' contemporaries thought that He might be one of the Old Testament prophets. He did not claim to be a prophet, but rather that He personally fulfilled one of the most important prophecies, that of the Prophet Isaiah. He did this in the synagogue of Nazareth, His home city.

So He came to Nazareth, where He had been brought up. And as His custom was, He went into the synagogue on the Sabbath day, and stood up to read. And He was handed the book of the prophet Isaiah. And when He had opened the book, He found the place where it was written:

> The Spirit of the Lord is upon Me,
>> Because He has anointed Me
> To preach the gospel to the poor; He has sent
>> Me to heal the brokenhearted,
> To proclaim liberty to the captives, and
>> recovery of sight to the blind,
> To set at liberty those who are oppressed;
>> To proclaim the acceptable year of the Lord.

> Then He closed the book and gave it back to the attendant and sat down. And the eyes of all who were in the synagogue were fixed on Him. And He began to say to them, "Today this Scripture is fulfilled in your hearing."

The people were shocked. "Is this not Joseph's son?" Jesus then says to them, "No prophet is accepted in his own country."

> And when they heard this they were filled with wrath and rose up and thrust Him out of the city. (Luke 4.16–29)

Another confrontation occurred when Jesus healed a crippled man at the Pool of Siloam, again on the Sabbath, and thus again incurred the wrath of the Jewish leaders.

> For this reason the Jews persecuted Jesus, and sought to kill Him, because He had done these things on the

Sabbath. But Jesus answered them, "My Father has been working until now, and I have been working." Therefore the Jews sought all the more to kill Him, because He not only broke the Sabbath, but also said that God was His Father, *making Himself equal with God*. (John 5.16–18)

The same accusation appeared when Jesus said that He and His Father were one.

Then the Jews took up stones again to stone Him. Jesus answered them, "Many good works I have shown you from My Father. For which of those works do you stone Me?" The Jews answered Him, saying, "For a good work we do not stone You, but for blasphemy, and because You, being a Man, make Yourself God." (John 10.30–33)

On numerous occasions Jesus insisted that He was sent by the Father to do His will. He knew the Father, for the Father and He were one. To see Him was to see the Father.

And no one could come to the Father except through Him.

"I am the way, the truth, and the life. No one comes to the Father except through Me. If you had known Me, you would have known My Father also; and from now on you know Him and have seen Him." Philip said to Him, "Lord, show us the Father, and it is sufficient for us." Jesus said to him, "Have I been with you so long, and yet you have not known Me, Philip? He who has seen Me has seen the Father; so how can you say, 'Show us the Father'? Do you not believe that I am in the Father, and the Father in Me? The words that I speak to you I do not speak on My own authority; but the Father who dwells in Me does the works. Believe Me that I am in the Father and the Father in Me, or else believe Me for the sake of the works themselves." (John 14.6–11)

Jesus admitted that He was both the Messiah and the Son of God. He further revealed that the Father and He were one. It was because of His identity that Jesus was rejected.

The Final Answer to His Identity

The most powerful statement made by Jesus regarding His identity appears in the eighth chapter of St John's Gospel. Jesus confronts His adversaries in the Jerusalem Temple. He tells them that because of their actions they were not really the children of Abraham. They accuse Jesus of being a Samaritan and having a demon. What troubled them was that Jesus was telling the people that anyone who kept His word would not see death. Jesus then tells them that Abraham had rejoiced to see His day. The Jews then responded, *You are not fifty years old, and you have seen Abraham?* Could Jesus have said things more difficult for His adversaries? He could—and He did. At that point Jesus says something that shocked and horrified the Jews. His response was *Most assuredly, I say to you, before Abraham was I AM!* (John 8.58).

Abraham lived 1800 years before Christ. Here Jesus is saying that He was alive in the time of Abraham, and that Abraham both saw Him and rejoiced. The final two words of the answer of Jesus were either true, or they were the height of blasphemy. Jesus did not say, "I was"; He said, "I AM."

The Jews had heard those words before. They were to be found in the Book of Exodus. *There were no more important words in the Torah.* They were spoken to Moses when God spoke to him at the Burning Bush. God told Abraham that he was to lead the people out of Egypt. Moses then asked a daring but understandable question.

Then Moses said to God, "Indeed, when I come to the children of Israel and say to them, 'The God of your fathers has sent me to you,' and they say to me, 'What is His name?' what shall I say to them?" "And God said to Moses, "I AM THAT I AM." And He said, "Thus you shall say to the children of Israel, 'I AM hath sent me unto you.'" (Exodus 3.13–14 KJV)

This is God's Name.

Jesus had just claimed to be the One who spoke to Moses. Jesus had claimed to be the Messiah and the Son of God. He and the Father were One. With these words Jesus was claiming to be the Divine Person who spoke to Moses.

Was Jesus a madman or who He says He was? Believing that He was a nice teacher, or someone who went about doing good, or simply someone who taught the brotherhood of man, simply does not face up to what He said about Himself. Either dismiss Him or accept Him. There is no possible word in the English language to describe Him if he were other than a Divine Person. To call Him a lunatic or a deranged person does not even come close. Either He is to be completely rejected, or worshipped as God.

Why Was Jesus Crucified?

As we know, Jesus was rejected by the religious leaders. He was not condemned for what He did. *He was sent to His death because of His identity and specifically who He claimed to be.* Jesus appeared before both the Jewish Sanhedrin and Pontius Pilate who represented the Roman Empire. In both situations it was His identity that was in question.

The trial of Jesus begins:

As soon as it was day, the elders of the people, both chief priests and scribes, came together and led Him into their council, saying, "If You are the Christ, tell us." But He said to them, "If I tell you, you will by no means believe. And if I also ask you, you will by no means answer Me or let Me go. Hereafter the Son of Man will sit on the right hand of the power of God." Then they all said, "Are You then the Son of God?" So He said to them, "You rightly say that I am." And they said, "What further testimony do we need? For we have heard it ourselves from His own mouth." (Luke 22.66–71)

Again the high priest asked Him, saying to Him, "Are You the Christ, the Son of the Blessed?" Jesus said, "I am. And you will see the Son of Man sitting at the right hand of the Power, and coming with the clouds of heaven." Then the high priest tore his clothes and said, "What further need do we have of witnesses? You have heard

the blasphemy! What do you think?" And they all condemned Him to be deserving of death. (Mark 14.62–64)

Jesus was sent to Pilate.

Then they led Jesus from Caiaphas to the Praetorium,
and it was early morning. But they themselves did not
go into the Praetorium, lest they should be defiled, but
that they might eat the Passover. Pilate then went out to
them and said, "What accusation do you bring against
this Man?" They answered and said to him, "If He were
not an evildoer, we would not have delivered Him up to
you." Then Pilate said to them, "You take Him and judge
Him according to your law." Therefore the Jews said to
him, "It is not lawful for us to put anyone to death," that
the saying of Jesus might be fulfilled which He spoke,
signifying by what death He would die.

Then Pilate entered the Praetorium again, called
Jesus, and said to Him, "Are You the king of the Jews?"
Jesus answered him, "Are you speaking for yourself about
this, or did others tell you this concerning Me?" Pilate
answered, "Am I a Jew? Your own nation and the chief
priests have delivered You to me. What have You done?"
Jesus answered, "My kingdom is not of this world. If My

kingdom were of this world, My servants would fight, so that I should not be delivered to the Jews; but now My kingdom is not from here." Pilate therefore said to Him, "Are You a king then?" Jesus answered, "You say rightly that I am a king. For this cause I was born, and for this cause I have come into the world, that I should bear witness to the truth. Everyone who is of the truth hears My voice." (John 18.28–37)

Before the Jewish court and the Roman governor the central issue was the identity of Jesus. It was for His identity that He was crucified.

Why Did Jesus Come? What Did He Do?

The most common answer to the question "Why did Jesus come?" will probably be "to save." *Save* has a least two meanings. We can say that the doctor saved the man's life from cancer. We can say "he saved his money for a new car." When we say that Jesus saved us, which do we mean? Did He save us *from* something? Or did He save us *for* something? The answer is both. He saved us from something and for something.

I will answer for myself and for my life experience. I believe that I need to be saved. The first thing that I need to be saved from is death. Is death the end? Is there life after death? One thing is for sure: no matter how good my health is, or how good my doctors are, my life will end. Nothing can change that for me or for anyone else. If there is anything beyond this life, nothing in this world can make that happen.

But there is something else that I need to be saved from. As I have lived my life, I have had experiences of what we call evil. It comes in various forms. It could be in a physical form, such as a death-dealing disease. Cancer is a physical evil. I have experienced evil in my own life. I have seen behavior in other people that is unfair, cruel, and ugly. Evil is something that goes beyond bad taste.

I had an experience of this when I visited a place called Mauthausen in Austria. It was a death camp that the Austrians have preserved with all its horrors. As I walked in the rooms where the atrocities were carried out, some with pictures of those inhuman acts, I had a very strong sense of evil. What I experienced was something beyond human weakness. It was diabolic. Some in our world would dismiss the existence of demons as fantasy. But there have been too many instances of their presence to discount their activity in the world. The Catholic Church has about 135 exorcists working in the United States. My advice is to stay away from anything that is even remotely associated with the demonic.

One thing I have learned in life is that despite how hard you try, evil never makes sense. We may ask why people do certain evil things or why evil things happen, but we will never have a satisfactory answer. Our minds were made for beauty and truth. To live in evil is to live in darkness. We become blind to the truth. To remain in this darkness is to lose the meaning of our life. The world of 2023 is as much in need of deliverance as has been every age in human history. I too need to be saved. Humanity needs to be saved from both evil and death, even though the secular world accepts evil and death as simply "natural." The "natural" world ended the day Adam left paradise. If we need to be saved from evil and death, we must consider their source.

What Is the Source of Evil?

Why are things this way? Is man naturally evil? To the secularist, evil and death may seem to be perfectly normal. That is how things are, so deal with it! I am not sure who exactly wrote the Book of Genesis, but whoever wrote it was a genius.

It is the famous story of Adam and Eve. It is an analysis of the whole question of good, evil, and death. The author begins by telling us that we live in a world that has a Creator, a personal one. Secondly, he tells us that the world He created was good. This is repeated six times, *And God saw that it was good.* Perhaps this was to make sure we get the point.

God then creates this monogamous couple. They live in Paradise. They live with God. God talks to them. He gives them authority over all living things. And then He gives them the commandment *not* to eat the fruit of one tree. If they eat of this fruit, they will die. They do not obey and eat the forbidden fruit. They have sinned. They are expelled from the garden. They no longer live in unity with God. Although they did not physically die on that day, God told them that when they ate of it, they would die. They did not lose their physical life at that point, but they lost the life they shared with God. Death was the direct result of sin. They died spiritually. The author makes the point that this was not God's doing; it was man's. This event is known as *the Fall.*

One point must be made. Creation is one thing, the Fall is another. The world we live in today bears some of the goodness and beauty of the original creation, but it is fallen. God did not make evil. Evil is the result of the Fall.

The Genesis story is the most plausible one that I have ever come across. It gets to the heart of the matter. It explains the battle between good and evil that goes on in each of our lives. It was truly inspired. If the condition of man and the creation was caused by Adam, a second and *new Adam would be needed to restore man to God.* The world needed a fresh start. The Second Adam would have to undo the whole "sin and death" catastrophe. More than bringing about God's forgiveness, the Second Adam would have to overcome both sin and death. We lost the life given to Adam by God. Only God could restore it.

Thankfully there is a "Second Adam" and He is Jesus Christ. St Paul tells us:

> The first man Adam became a living being. The last Adam became a life-giving spirit. However, the spiritual is not first, but the natural, and afterward the spiritual. The first man was of the earth, made of dust; the second Man is the Lord from heaven. As was the man of dust, so also are those who are made of dust; and as is the heavenly Man, so also are those who are heavenly. And as we have borne the image of the man of dust, we shall also bear the image of the heavenly Man. (1 Corinthians 15.45–49)

The task of the Second Adam is to bring us back to unity with God, and secondly to overcome both sin and death. And that is what the life of Christ is about. That is what Christianity is about. That is why it is called the *Gospel* or "Good News," as we read the announcement of the birth of Christ to the frightened shepherds, *Do not be afraid, for behold, I bring you good tidings of great joy which will be to all people. For there is born to you this day in the city of David a Savior, who is Christ the Lord* (Luke 2.10). The Gospel begins with the joy proclaimed by the angels and ends with joy of the two disciples who met Jesus on the road to Emmaus. After meeting the risen Christ, the two men *returned to Jerusalem with great joy* (Luke 24.50). One of the most tragic accusations against Christians is that they have no joy.

He has come to save us *from* sin and death, and *for* the life lost by Adam. Jesus was the only one who could do this. He could do it because He was both human and divine, united in One Person. In Him the life of God and the life of man were brought back together. This occurred the moment He was conceived in the womb of His Mother. This is what we profess by praying the Creed in church. If there is any possibility that we may have that life, it can only be by some way being united to Him. Apart from Him, it would seem that the cemetery is our last stop. This life becomes possible through the Church.

How Are We Saved?

How then does Jesus save us from the mystery of sin and death? Adam was told that on the day when he ate the forbidden fruit, he would die. But he didn't, at least not physically. That would come later. But, in fact, he did die. The life he shared with God was finished. He endured a spiritual death. And that death is our inheritance. St Augustine, the great theologian of the Western (Catholic) Church, mistakenly taught that we inherit the *guilt* of Adam. (He had a bad translation of the New Testament.) We do not share Adam's guilt. We are not born guilty; we are born in the condition of Adam when he was expelled from Paradise. We are born in need of restoration to God and to be freed from the consequences of sin and death. We need a Redeemer.

Although we are aware of evil and death, real evil is incomprehensible. It does not make sense. Evil does not belong in our world. It is repugnant. The demonic power that existed before Christ has been broken. But it is still present in a weakened condition.

Those who commit great acts of evil are separated from society, sometimes even by being put to death. All that being said, even though we do not completely understand it, evil is present. The second great mystery is death. None of us has been there. It is the great unknown, but it awaits all mankind.

How did Jesus overcome this great double mystery of evil and death? Here I would note that although the Church has defined who Jesus is, it has not spelled out in specific details how His death and Resurrection have changed things. The response to that question is found in the prayers and hymns of the Church.

The most evil act ever done by man was crucifying Christ. That was not just an act of murder. *It was an act of deicide.* The One who was both human and divine was put to death. This was the summit of evil.

In willingly enduring the crucifixion, Jesus entered into the mystery of both evil and death. He was perfectly sinless. He was Life itself. By embracing evil and death, Jesus overpowered them. The Apostles' Creed states, "He suffered under Pontius Pilate, was crucified, died, and was buried. He descended into hades." There is a beautiful icon that shows Christ in the realm of death breaking down its doors and bringing Adam and Eve out of death.

At Easter we sing, "Christ is risen from the dead, trampling down death by (His) death." Jesus rose from the dead as the Conqueror of death. At that moment the power of evil and death over mankind was broken "at least in the human and divine Jesus Christ." That is what Easter is about. It is why Easter is the greatest Christian feast. Orthodox Christians do not say, "Happy Easter." They say, "Christ is risen!" The person greeted then responds by saying "Truly He is risen!"

We can say that if salvation means that the restoration of the Life of God to man has been achieved, and the power of sin and death have been conquered in Christ—we may say that salvation is an accomplished fact. But how does all this affect us? Jesus proclaimed, *I did not come to call the righteous, but sinners* (Mark 2.17). *For God did not send His Son into the world to judge the world, but that the world might through him be saved* (John 3.17).

If we are to be saved, we need to be united to Christ so that what was accomplished in Him is available to us. This is His promise to us. This is what He says about that life. *As the Father has life in Himself, He has given it to the Son to have life in Himself* (John 5.26). *Indeed, just as the Father raises the dead and grants life, so the Son grants life to those to whom He will* (John 5.21). *I came that they may have life and have it to the full*

(John 10.10). *I am the living bread that came down from heaven.
If anyone eats of this bread, he will live forever. And the bread
that I will give for the life of the world is My flesh* (John 6.51). *I
am the way the truth and the life, and no one comes to the Father
except through Me* (John 14.6). *I am the resurrection and the life*
(John 11.25). *Come to Me that you may have life* (John 5.40).

In his First Letter St John makes all this very clear. *God
gave us eternal life and this life is in His Son. He who has the Son
possesses life. Whoever does not have the Son of God does not have
life* (1 John 5.12). All mankind is in need of a saving relationship with Jesus Christ. But how do we achieve this?

In order for us to share the life promised by Christ, something has to happen to us. If we are to share in this mystery of
salvation, we must be united to Christ in a way that is more
than psychological. That is what He told the elderly Nicodemus who came to Jesus at night. Jesus told him that he had to
be "reborn." This shocked Nicodemus who insisted that this
would be physically impossible. Jesus then told him that he
had to be born again of water and the Holy Spirit. Jesus was
talking about Baptism. *It is through Baptism that we are united
to Christ and share in His Life.*

4

The Church

Do We Really Need It?

Why Are Baptism and the Sacraments Important?

The word "baptism" comes from the Greek word "to immerse." In the early Church, Baptism was by done immersing the person into the water three times. By going down into the water and coming out, being baptized was seen as reenacting of the death and Resurrection of Christ.

Is Baptism real or "symbolic?" Many people continue to ask that question. St Paul explained it to the Romans:

> Do you not know that all of us who have been baptized
> into Christ Jesus were baptized into his death? We were

buried therefore with him by baptism into death, so that as Christ was raised from the dead by the glory of the Father, we too might walk in newness of life. For if we have been united with him in a death like his, we shall certainly be united with him in a resurrection like his. We know that our old self was crucified with him so that the sinful body might be destroyed, and we might no longer be enslaved to sin. For he who has died is freed from sin. But if we have died with Christ, we believe that we shall also live with him. For we know that Christ being raised from the dead will never die again; death no longer has dominion over him. The death he died he died to sin, once for all, but the life he lives he lives to God. So you also must consider yourselves dead to sin and alive to God in Christ Jesus. (Romans 6.3–11)

In Ephesians 2.5 we are told that "He made us alive together with Christ."

And He said to them, *Go into all the world and preach the gospel to every creature. Whoever believes and is baptized will be saved, but whoever does not believe will be condemned* (Mark 16.16). The new and eternal life was given to each person when he or she was baptized.

For fourteen centuries the Church taught that this saving relationship with Christ was achieved through faith and Baptism. Every baptized person was seen as a "born again Christian." During the Protestant Reformation in the 1500s, one group of Protestants rejected this teaching. They said or claimed that Baptism had no real effect on the person being baptized. The saving relationship was brought about only by the faith of the person. And since the person would have to be of a certain age to make an act of faith, the Baptism of infants was rejected. They practiced so-called "believers' baptism." That is the position of Evangelical Christians today. Historically they were insisting that salvation did not come "by works" but only "by faith." They took this concept to the extreme. Consequently even Baptism did not count. This radically changed their understanding of the other sacraments and of the Church itself. Rather than being a divine institution capable of uniting a person to Christ through its sacraments, the Church was simply a community of people who believed in Christ.

Jesus also said that his followers must be born again of water—and the Holy Spirit. The Church understood that this occurred when the candidate was anointed immediately after Baptism. It came to be known as Confirmation in the

Catholic Church and Chrismation in the Orthodox Church. Baptism and Confirmation were separated in the Catholic Church. Confirmation was given when the child was older. The Orthodox Church chrismated (i.e., confirmed) the newly baptized child and immediately gave him or her Holy Communion—and still does.

The Eucharist

Given the importance of the Eucharist in the life of the Church, something should be said about the question of intercommunion. The Orthodox Church does not practice "open communion." This has nothing to do with the worthiness of the communicant. It has to do with Faith. The Eucharist is a celebration of our unity of Faith. We can celebrate our unity of Faith only if in fact the unity exists. When someone comes forward to receive Communion that person is saying, "I share your Faith, I am part of this communion of Faith." "Closed communion" was the practice of the Catholic Church until recently.

Vatican II addressed the question in 1964 in the decree *Orientalium Ecclesiarum*. The bishops believed that there were situations in which Catholics and Orthodox might receive the sacraments of Penance, Anointing, and the Eucharist in each other's churches.

> Eastern Christians who are separated in good faith from the Catholic Church, if they are rightly disposed and make such a request of their own accord, may be given the Sacraments of Penance, the Eucharist and the Anointing of the sick. Moreover, Catholics may also ask for the same sacraments from non-Catholic ministers in whose church there are valid sacraments, as often as necessity or true spiritual benefit recommends such action, and access to a Catholic priest is physically or morally impossible. (*Orientalium Ecclesiarum* 27)

Canon 844 of the Catholic Code of Canon Law allows for this same practice of inter-communion. As noted above, the Orthodox Church does not allow it.

At the present time, among many, questionable practices are occurring. The Catholic bishops and priests in Germany have advocated and practiced inter-communion with Protestants. This practice undermines the theology of both the Eucharist and the Church. It is not without reason that the Church refers to the Eucharist as "Holy *Communion*."

The Sacrament of Marriage

Both Orthodoxy and Catholicism regard Marriage as one of the sacraments. The pastoral problem facing both Churches is the number of people who have been divorced from their spouses and who have either have entered or wish to enter into a second marriage. The Catholic Church has found a way to restore those Catholics by declaring that something was lacking in the first marriage to the extent that the Church gives a "declaration of nullity." This is not an annulment of a marriage—but rather a statement that the first marriage lacked something fundamental to marriage, a lack that allows the Church to make this declaration of nullity—in effect to declare that no real marriage existed from the outset. This will obviously seem strange after many years of marriage and several children.

The Orthodox Church has a different pastoral approach. There is no denying the reality of the first marriage if it was performed by the Church. But in many cases the relationship between the husband and wife has irreparably broken down. In such cases the diocesan bishop may permit a second marriage for the sake of their salvation. The second marriage service is more subdued and has a penitential tone. In some

Orthodox jurisdictions a couple converting to Orthodoxy may be asked to receive the sacrament of Marriage in the Orthodox Church. Catholics in a second marriage who enter Orthodoxy can be fully restored to the sacraments.

Summary

Permit me to summarize what I have been saying. The truth of the Christian Faith depends completely on the identity of Jesus Christ. He claimed to be the Messiah and the Son of God. He even went so far as to claim that He existed before Abraham, who saw His days. He then claimed the Divine Name spoken to Moses, "I AM." Jesus is either who He says He is, or He is a liar or a mad man. Like St Peter, a Christian must confess that He is the Christ, the Son of the Living God. Jesus was proclaimed as Savior by the angels. As Savior he has restored what Adam lost, the life of God. He has overcome the condition of evil and death that came about as the result of Adam's sin. Through His cross and Resurrection, He has overcome sin and death. He now wishes to share with mankind the Life given to Him by the Father. He does this through Baptism and Confirmation [Chrismation]. This happens in the life of the Church. Let us now look at the reality of the Church.

What Is the Importance of the Church?

Jesus made a number of promises to his disciples before His Ascension. He promised that He would be with them always, until the end of the world (Matthew 28.20). He also made three specific promises that reveal His continued care for the Church. These promises have to do with the Holy Spirit. He promised that He would ask the Father to send the Holy Spirit upon His disciples. The Holy Spirit would guide them in all truth. The Holy Spirit would be with them forever. He fulfilled these promises on the day of Pentecost, fifty days after His Resurrection. These texts may be found in the Gospel according to St John (14.12–25 and 16.12–15). These promises and the gift of the Holy Spirit at Pentecost reveal that the Church is something more than a group of people who believe in Jesus. His disciples live in unity with Christ and the Holy Spirit. The Holy Spirit would lead them in all Truth and would be with them until the end of the world. The Church was and is a living organism united to the Three Persons of the Godhead.

As we look into New Testament documents beyond the four Gospels, they affirm that the Church is something more than a human institution. The Church is called *the Body of Christ* (Ephesians 1.22–24). It is called the *Bride of Christ* (Revelation 21.9). It is called the *Church of the Living God* (1 Timothy 3.15). It is called the *flock of Christ* (1 Peter 5.2). It is called *God's building* (1 Corinthians 3.9). It is called *the temple of the Living God* (2 Corinthians 6.16). Finally it is called *the pillar and ground of truth* (1 Timothy 3.15).

Each of these titles not only refers to the *human* community that constitutes the Church on earth but also contains a reference to another element in the Church, the *divine*. The Church, like Christ Himself, is both human and divine. And as the human and divine Christ was one, so too is the Church. There is no "mystical Church" apart from the earthly Church.

The Church is human. It is made up of people who are in the process of being saved. They are capable of sin. That is true even of those who hold positions of authority in the Church. Judas Iscariot betrayed Jesus. St Peter three times denied even knowing Him. Unfortunately, we should never be surprised when members of the Church fail to live up to the demands of the Gospel.

The Church has its Divine Element. God does not aban-
don the Church even when church leaders fail us. Back in
the third century the Church faced a similar problem. People
asked their bishops, "What is my standing in the Church? I
was baptized by a sinful priest. Is my Baptism invalid?" The
Church answered, "No!" An unworthy minister cannot block
the grace (God's Life) of God. Through Baptism and the
other sacraments the Church is still the source of God's Truth
and Life. It is still the Body of Christ and the Temple of the
Holy Spirit. As some people could only see the human Christ,
some today can see only a human Church. When we pray the
Creed, we confess our faith in the Church as one, holy, catholic, and apostolic.

But Which Church?

Today there are countless denominations. This is not the will
of Christ, who prayed that *they all may be one* (John 17.21).
My intent here is not to judge others who differ from us, but
to clarify the beliefs and practices that divide us. From the
perspective of the historic Church, to be a Christian, one has
to have faith in Jesus Christ and be baptized in water in the
name of the Father, Son, and Holy Spirit.

Jehovah's Witnesses do not believe in the Trinity or in the full divinity of Christ. The belief of the Mormons is also problematic. They believe that God the Father had flesh and bones. They do not believe in the Trinity as traditional Christians do. Those who have never been baptized lack something essential to full membership. *He who believes and is baptized will be saved* (Mark 16.16).

Do these words mean that people who have never heard of Christ will be denied heaven? It is true that Jesus Christ is one with the Father. There is no other way to the Father. The Church opens that path to the baptized. We know that God has been revealed as a loving Father. Can the Father unite others to Christ when they die? We can say that God "stands behind" the sacraments, but His hands are not bound by them. Some things must be left to God.

Today it is very difficult to know what various Protestant denominations believe. Most have moved away from their historical "confessions of faith." Some baptize in the name of the Creator, Redeemer, and Sanctifier. Many believe that Holy Communion is nothing more than bread and wine. Much depends on the opinions of the local pastor.

If we judge an individual Church by its historical roots, three Churches can claim to be "apostolic" or existing from the days of the Apostles. These are the Catholic Church of Rome, the Orthodox Churches in the East, and those referred to as "Oriental Orthodox" (the Coptic Church of Egypt, the Church of Armenia, the Syriac Church of the Middle East, the Ethiopian Orthodox Church, and the Church of India). These churches all profess *almost* the same faith. They are sacramental Churches with bishops and priests, and they honor the Virgin Mary and the saints. They pray for the dead.

All Christians who believe in the divinity of Christ believe that all men are in need of a saving relationship with Jesus Christ. Protestants agree, but they differ on how one becomes united to Christ. For them salvation comes only "by faith." The sacramental Churches believe that this unity comes about by faith and Baptism. Because the Church is the Body of Christ, it is itself the New Life brought by Christ.

St John teaches this in the first chapter of his Gospel. *And of His fullness we have all received, and grace for grace. For the law was given through Moses, but grace and truth came through Jesus Christ. No one has seen God at any time. The only begotten Son, who is in the bosom of the Father, He has declared Him* (1 John 1.18).

The Church "ministers" the Grace (Divine Life) and Truth of Christ to the world. Here we are not talking about operating soup kitchens to address the physical hunger of people. By being baptized and becoming members of the Church we share in Eternal Life. The sacraments of the Church minister that Life. We can admire the faith of Evangelical Christians who insist on personal faith in Christ. But their understanding of the Church is different. They do not see how bread and wine can be the Body and Blood of Christ, nor how the Church can minister the forgiveness of God. They believe in the Holy Spirit, but they do not see the continuity of the Holy Spirit in the historic and apostolic Church as do Catholics and Orthodox.

In his Second Epistle St Peter speaks to the "people of faith." He tells them of their new identity.

> Grace and peace be multiplied to you in the knowledge of God and of Jesus our Lord, as His divine power has given to us all things that *pertain* to life and godliness, through the knowledge of Him who called us by glory and virtue, by which have been given to us exceedingly great and precious promises, that through *these you may be partakers of the divine nature,* having escaped the corruption *that is* in the world through lust. (2 Peter 1.2–4)

Being a Christian means to share in the New Life of Christ. It is so real that St Peter speaks of it as a partaking *of the divine nature.* That is very strong language. That is God's gift. As a consequence, the Church is very important.

Where do we find it? The Protestant movement was founded in the sixteenth century. The Church of Rome, the Orthodox Church, and the non-Chalcedonian Churches date back to the Apostles. These three are similar to each other in many ways. They are hierarchical—that is, they have bishops, priests and deacons. They have monks and nuns. They are sacramental. They honor the Mother of God and the saints. I will limit my following remarks to the Church of Rome and the Orthodox Church.

5

The Choice of Orthodoxy

Could I Be a Part of It?

The Undivided Church?

From apostolic times, there were small groups who separated from the Universal Church over various theological views. In the fifth century the Church of Alexandria, the Armenians, the Ethiopians, the Syriac Church, and the Churches of Mesopotamia and India broke communion with the other Churches either over the issue of calling Mary the Theotokos as defended by the Council of Ephesus (Nestorians) or over the theology of the Council of Chalcedon, which defined the two natures in the One Person of Christ (these are referred to as the non-Chalcedonian Churches). Although it is difficult to speak of the "undivided Church," the term usually means the Church in which Rome and Constantinople were one.

The Church was founded in Jerusalem. Christianity is a Middle Eastern religion. Many of the Churches in the Middle East and Asia Minor were founded in the first century by the apostles. The Church of Rome also dates from the first century. The claim that its origins go back to Saint Peter and Paul is almost universally accepted. Jews were either brought to Rome or came willingly in the first century. It was from among them that the Christian community arose. It came to be called the "apostolic see" in the writings of Pope Damasus I (366–384) because it was the *only Church in the Western Roman Empire that was actually founded by apostles.* In fact in the East many of the Churches were apostolic. In time, five Churches were called patriarchal Churches: Jerusalem, Antioch, Rome, Alexandria, and Constantinople.

The papal claims are based upon the presence of St Peter in Rome, but Peter was first in Jerusalem. His presence and that of St Paul in Antioch are well documented in the New Testament. Yet neither Jerusalem nor Antioch claimed supremacy over all other Churches.

The bishops of Rome claimed to be the heirs of St Peter. The use of the word *heir* is important. In Roman Law, the heir inherited not only the property and debts of the one who named him his heir; he inherited also the rights and duties of the deceased.

St Leo the Great, pope of Rome from 440 to 461, was a champion of Roman supremacy. He affirmed that he personally was not a greater Christian than others, *but as bishop of Rome he was the embodiment of St Peter, inheriting from him the power and authority that Christ endowed him with in the Gospel.*

In the first millennium the popes, as bishops of Rome, came to be very important in the life of the entire Church. When compared with the christological heresies that arose in the East, the Church of Rome was seen as very orthodox. The pope did not assert authority over the Eastern Church before the Schism of 1054.

1054 Schism—or Schisms? What Separated Us?

The Schism of 1054 has lasted nearly a thousand years. It is the most important schism between the Catholic Church and the East, *but it was not the first or only schism* between the Church of Rome and the Eastern Churches.

Confusion about who was the rightful bishop of Antioch caused the Meletian Schism which lasted from 360 to 418.

This was primarily an issue for the Eastern Churches, but eventually the Church of Rome became involved. The Acacian Schism lasted from 484 to 519. This was a schism between Pope Felix III of Rome and Patriarch Acacius of Constantinople. The schism between Rome and Patriarch Photios, known as the Photian Schism, lasted from 863 to 869. In time these schisms were resolved. Did either see that the other ceased to be the One, Holy, Catholic, and Apostolic Church? The Schism of 1054 remains unresolved despite the efforts of the Council of Ferrara-Florence in the fifteenth century. The results of the council were not accepted in the East.

The Schism of 1054 occurred during a time of change and centralization in the Church in the West. The era was marked by two reform movements. The first was the monastic reform carried out by the monks of Cluny. The second was the Gregorian reform of Pope Gregory VII. Gregory's reform occurred immediately after the Schism of 1054. Pope Leo IX, the pope of the schism, carried out a reform against simony and clerical marriage. He personally led an army into Italy against the Normans who had established themselves in the South of Italy and were encroaching on papal lands, but who, ironically, were ecclesiastically faithful to the papacy.

The Normans had been forcing the Byzantine Churches in the South Italian domains they had recently conquered to conform to the practices of the Latin Church, which included a celibate clergy. The patriarch of Constantinople reacted by closing the Latin churches there. Other troublesome issues were raised by the Eastern Church: the use of unleavened bread, the claim that the Holy Spirit proceeds from the Father and from the Son (the Filioque), and the claims of the papacy. To resolve the problems a papal delegation was sent to Constantinople, with Cardinal Humbert of Silva Candida at its head. He carried papal letters that he himself had written.

Unfortunately the two men who were to resolve the problems were personally ill-equipped to deal with the issues. Cardinal Humbert, representing Rome, intended to confront the patriarch. The patriarch of Constantinople, Michael Cerularius, was as stubborn as Cardinal Humbert. They excommunicated each other. Pope Leo IX was already dead at this time, and thus the excommunication had no real canonical status. Did either Church see the gravity of these events?

Scholars today do not regard the events of 1054 as the definitive break between the Catholic and the Orthodox Churches. The Orthodox canonist John H. Erickson noted over fifty years ago, "As the amount of ink and parchment expended would indicate, for most Byzantine churchmen of the 11th and 12th centuries the principal point of disagreement was not papal primacy or Filioque but rather the use of unleavened bread in the Eucharist."[4]

The event that irreparably damaged the relationship between the two Churches was the Fourth Crusade in 1204. The Western Crusaders from Venice conquered Constantinople, imposing all the horrors that accompany such destruction. Every abomination was committed. *There is no more tragic event in the history of the Church.* A Catholic emperor and a Catholic bishop were imposed on the city. After seventy-five years the Greeks retook the city, but things were never the same. In the minds of the Orthodox the tragedy of 1204 is as memorable as the attack on Pearl Harbor is in the minds of Americans. A very deep bitterness remained in the hearts of the Greek Christian people. In 1453 Constantinople fell to the Turks. The great Church of Holy Wisdom became a mosque. Imagine how the people of Rome would feel if St Peter's became a mosque. In the past half century the

---

[4] John H. Erickson, "Leavened and Unleavened: Some Theological Implications of the Schism of 1054," *St Vladimir's Theological Quarterly* 14.3 (1970): 155–176, at 157.

pope and the patriarch of Constantinople have met in friendly meetings. Pope John Paul II even apologized to the Greeks. But the role of the bishop of Rome was and still is the *great dividing question* between the Western Catholics and the Eastern Orthodox. The Orthodox see the pope as the "first among equals," but not having jurisdiction over the entire Church.

The Present Era

When I look back to the Church where I served as a priest in the 1970s, I see that things have changed in many ways! When I served as an assistant pastor in 1970, there were over 1600 families in the parish. It had a very large elementary school. Near the parish was a regional Catholic high school. Today that parish is closed. The high school is also closed. I have heard that both properties have been sold. Recently the Archbishop of Detroit said that only half the people who claim to be Catholic are registered in a parish, and of those only 30% go to church. His math tells me that 85% of Catholics in his archdiocese no longer go to church. That does not bode well for the future.

From what I have said about secularism, there is little doubt that the large-scale falling off of church membership is in some measure due to this clash of cultures. Children educated in public schools, where one must remain silent about religious matters, are likely to form a secular identity. Modern colleges and universities are often places where the Christian Faith and church membership are ridiculed. Today they are places of indoctrination. They are no longer places of free thought and free speech. But these are external forces affecting church membership.

Secular forces against Christianity have always been present in the world, but in the past half century forces from within the Church have proved detrimental to its own faith. And in the years after Vatican Council II, especially in the 1970s and 1980s, a time of change and confusion became commonplace in Catholic parishes.

The heart of the matter was the disregard of Tradition. Tradition is the work of the Holy Spirit in the Church. The traditional music of the Church changed. Some really bad music was produced. The architecture of the churches, both interior and exterior, left people wondering what they were looking at. Many, although not all, priests took great liberties with the Mass and other services. Catholic people never knew what awaited them on Sunday morning. The old practice of finding the identical service in every Catholic church was history.

In some extreme instances, the effect of these changes was to turn a sacred rite into a theatrical production. Unfortunately those in charge were not very good at theater. The focus of the Church was no longer God, but man. The Mass was now a meal. The priest was a worship leader. The hierarchy may not have realized it, but they were not far from the ideas of the sixteenth-century Protestant reformer, Huldrych Zwingli. He insisted that the Mass was simply a commemorative meal, and not a sacrifice.

In the post-Vatican I years, the "glue" that held things together in the Catholic Church was the pope. The measure of people's Catholicity was whether they were "under Rome." In the constantly changing years of the 1960s and 1970s, many Catholic priests felt at liberty to change things. They had never been trained to revere the Holy Tradition of the Church. The result was liturgical chaos.

To be sure, modern Protestantism underwent many of the same problems. The so-called "worship wars" divided many Protestant churches. On the other hand, Orthodoxy, which had been using English in the liturgy since the 1930s, did not change the Divine Liturgy itself.

We live in confusing times. Today it is said that the largest denomination in the US is that of the "inactive Catholics."

Many are spiritually homeless. They are sheep without a shepherd. They are faced with a number of decisions. Should I go to back to church? Should I have my children baptized? Should I register in the local parish? Should I disregard some of the crazy cardinals in the Vatican? Should I turn a blind eye to all the "human" problems and abuses in the Church? For those who have faith but have ceased attending church and cannot find themselves returning, what choices do they have?

Where to Go?

Some Catholic laity attend the *novus ordo* or the post-Vatican-II liturgy. The Latin rite, if made available around the world, could still serve as a unifying factor for Catholics and could serve as the rite for all international gatherings. There is little likelihood that that will happen. Despite the efforts of Pope Benedict XVI, there is now open hostility to the use of the older rite.

Should you join a Protestant Church? The rise of the large non-denominational "mega-churches" suggests that there are many people searching for a church that teaches the fundamentals of the faith—but those churches are non-sacramental. They do not believe in the reality of God's Life available in the sacraments. Baptism for them is a symbolic act that effects nothing. They rarely speak of the life of the Church from the first until the sixteenth century when Martin Luther and the Reformers came on the scene. What happened to the promise that Jesus made in which the Holy Spirit would be given to lead the Church in all truth and to be with the Church forever?

The mainline Protestant churches vary from some who hold the traditional faith and morals to others who preach various forms of heterodoxy. We do not know exactly what they believe. Each pastor is effectively his own pope deciding on what is to be believed, how to worship, and what is acceptable Christian behavior or what is not. Many have accepted the values of the secular world.

How Is the Orthodox Church Different?

The Orthodox and the Catholic Churches were One Church for the first thousand years. They existed in the two halves of the ancient Roman Empire with the Greek East and the Latin West. Greek was the language of the New Testament and even the liturgical language of Rome until the late second century. Both Churches abided by the same apostolic faith. Both celebrated the same worship though in different ways.

In time each spoke in slightly different ways about the same Christ and how He saved the world.

But also, in time, significant differences arose between them. In the Eastern half of the Church priests were chosen from both celibate and married men. In the West the obligation of celibacy was imposed on all priests although it was not always strictly observed. In the sixth century the Nicene Creed was changed in the West by the addition of the word Filioque, which means "and from the Son." The original Creed states belief in the Holy Spirit who proceeds "from the Father." The Eastern Church, believing that the Holy Spirit guided the bishops who met in Ecumenical Councils and wrote the Creed, regarded this change as unacceptable.

What then are the differences between Rome and Orthodoxy? Today, the pope is willing to pray the Nicene Creed with the Orthodox patriarch without the word Filioque. This is certainly a concession on his part. This no longer seems an insurmountable difference between the two. The dogmas regarding the Assumption and Immaculate Conception of Mary were declared by the Catholic Church in modern times. The Orthodox Church has never dogmatized either of these teachings. Nonetheless, Orthodoxy celebrates the Dormition (Assumption) of Mary on August 15, as does the

Catholic Church, and her conception by the righteous Anna on December 9 (the Catholic Church celebrates the dogmatized event on December 8).

On December 8, 1854 Pope Pius IX defined the dogma of the Immaculate Conception. This dogma refers to the conception of Mary herself, and not to the Virgin Birth of Jesus Christ. The two most important teachings about Mary are that she is truly the Theotokos (God-bearer, Mother of God) and that she is ever virgin. One of the most ancient Orthodox prayers to Mary expresses what the Orthodox believe about Mary:

> It is truly meet to bless thee, O Theotokos, ever blessed and most pure and the Mother of our God. More honorable than the Cherubim and more glorious beyond compare than the Seraphim, without corruption thou gavest birth to God the Word; true Theotokos, we magnify thee.

This hymn makes it clear that the Orthodox Church shares with the Catholic Church a deep veneration of Mary. The doctrine of the Immaculate Conception, which states that Mary herself was conceived without the stain of original sin, is not a teaching of the Orthodox Church, and for a very good reason. This dogma was defined within the context of St Augustine's understanding of original sin. In his view each person was born inheriting the guilt of Adam. His Latin text of Romans 5.12 read in reference to Adam *in whom all have sinned*. The original Greek text should be translated *whereas all have sinned*.

In the Augustinian understanding, because of Adam's sin, we inherit a defect (original sin, concupiscence) which both renders us guilty (until Baptism) and gives us a propensity toward committing actual sin.

The East did not understand original sin in the same way that the Catholic Church did. It did not see the "guilt of Adam" as being passed down to each person. The dogma of the Immaculate Conception was simply not needed. In my opinion it is not a dividing issue. Today the most problematic difference between the two Churches is the papacy.

The Orthodox Church sees that the ministry of St Peter is exercised by each bishop in each diocese. The "keys of the Kingdom" are here in this world and not up in heaven. Each diocesan bishop has the authority to "bind and to loose." Each priest receives the authority to hear confessions from his bishop. The ordination of married men to the priesthood has been practiced in the East from the earliest days of the Church. Celibacy is not a dogma. It is a church rule.

Orthodoxy is very traditional. Its liturgy has remained virtually unchanged for centuries. The art (icons) in the Orthodox Church must conform to what is read in the Holy Scriptures. No human being can pose for an icon of Christ or the Virgin Mary. That is not true in Catholic art. Renaissance artists used women whom they knew to pose for Mary. The art of Orthodoxy is the art of the Church, not the art of the artist. Visitors looking at an icon in an Orthodox Church depicting something biblical will quickly recognize what they are seeing.

There is a stability of faith and morals in Orthodoxy. What you read in the Scriptures, what you profess in the Creed, what you see in an icon, is all the same truth.

The Orthodox Church is the Church of saints and martyrs. In the last century more than twelve million Christians were killed by the Soviet government, and of these more than one hundred thousand were priests. Many Orthodox Christians lost their lives in the Balkans and the Middle East. As the late Fr Thomas Hopko stated in a class I attended, "Orthodox history is written in blood."

Does Orthodoxy have problems? Of course it does. The human element in the Church is always capable of wrongdoing. In the early centuries the heresies that denied the divinity or humanity of Christ had to be faced and rejected. Within Orthodoxy those problems are in the past, but human issues always arise in parishes and dioceses.

The stability of the Orthodox Church in matters of faith, morals, and worship is attractive. Many Protestants have become Orthodox in recent years. Most seek a Church that has been present since the Apostles, that teaches the same historical Faith expressed in the Creed, that celebrates a God-centered worship, and that does not change its moral beliefs with each new generation. Some Catholics have become Orthodox, but not nearly as many. One exception is in Central America where a very large number of people have become Orthodox. I believe that for Catholic people, no matter how they might feel about the pope, they can't imagine the Catholic Church without him. The current situation in Rome may be changing that.

Unfortunately, many Catholic people, including the clergy, simply do not know very much about Orthodoxy. In 1995 Pope John Paul II wrote an apostolic letter entitled *Orientale Lumen* (Light from the East), in which he encourages

Catholic people to learn about the Eastern Church. He suggested that this would enable the Church to "breathe with both lungs, East and West." Historically most arguments in defense of the Catholic faith have been against the Protestants. When one brings up those arguments with the Orthodox, they simply do not work. I have noticed over the past forty years that Catholic clergy tend to stay away from the Orthodox. If you wish to know about Orthodoxy, talk to the Orthodox.

If a person believes that Jesus Christ is the true Son of God and the Second Person of the Blessed Trinity and realizes that to be a Christian one has to be part of the Body of Christ, the Church, then that person should make a choice and become part of a parish. That choice should be made prayerfully and with very serious thought.

What Does Orthodoxy Offer?

Orthodoxy is the Church that has been present since Pentecost. It has the entire sacramental life. It baptizes children as infants. When it does, the newly baptized receive the sacraments of Chrismation (Confirmation) and the Holy Eucharist in the same ceremony. It has the sacraments of

Reconciliation (Confession), Matrimony, and Holy Orders. Its bishops trace their office to the Apostles. Orthodox people find their bishops closer to the laity than do the Catholic their bishops. It has priests and deacons. It has sufficient priests to serve even small parishes. Some men discover their vocation only later in life, after they have a wife and family. This does not prevent them from becoming priests. It has the monastic life for men and women. It has a treasury of art in the holy icons. Its churches range from the most humble to the magnificent.

Orthodoxy celebrates the same great feasts as the Catholic Church. It has the same liturgical seasons. It regards Advent as a lenten period. It also has a period of fasting before the feast of Sts Peter and Paul and before the Dormition of the Theotokos on August 15. It regards all the saints who died before the Schism of 1054 as saints. (Any Orthodox Irishmen can celebrate St Patrick's Day.)

Does Orthodoxy Have the Fullness of the Church?

Does it have the fullness of the Church? Catholic apologists insist that without the papacy, Orthodoxy lacks that fullness. Here we are speaking about the ministry given to St Peter by

Christ. The Petrine ministry is exercised *by all the bishops* of the Church. They "bind and loose." *If each diocese is truly a Church in its fullness, then it must contain all that is necessary for salvation.* All essential ministries must be present.

Mary is honored in the Orthodox Church by some of the most beautiful prayers. Most famous is the Akathist. In virtually every Orthodox Church her icon is most visible in the upper apse. Her place in the mystery of salvation is central and critical. It was she who gave our humanity to the Second Person of the Trinity. The faithful of the Orthodox Church also honor the saints and pray for the dead.

The worship of Orthodoxy centers on the Divine Liturgy (the Mass). It has the same fundamental components as the Western Rite, i.e., the Liturgy of the Word and the Liturgy of the Eucharist, but it has litanies and prayers not contained in the Latin Rite. It is longer than the current Catholic Mass. Each of the three Divine Liturgies used in the Orthodox Church, the Liturgy of St John Chrysostom, the Liturgy of St Basil the Great, and the Liturgy of St James, all specially speak of the Liturgy as a sacrifice. Although the Liturgy of St James is not used in the typical parish church, its text is readily available, and it is well worth reading. It contains some of the most majestic prayers ever written.

In the Divine Liturgy we become part of the most perfect act of worship, that of the sacrificial death and Resurrection of Christ. As prefigured by the ancient high priests of Israel in their temple worship, Jesus enters the true Holy of Holies with His own blood, making the perfect act of atonement. In the Divine Liturgy, the priests pray, "Thine own, of Thine own, we offer unto Thee on behalf of all and for all." There is an old Latin maxim: *Lex orandi est lex credendi,* which means the law of prayer is the law of belief. The faith of Orthodoxy is found in its prayers.

Do Orthodox Christians Believe in the Real Presence?

The Orthodox belief in the presence of Christ in the Eucharist is expressed in the prayer recited before receiving Communion. "I believe and I confess that thou art truly the Christ, the Son of the living God, who camest into the world to save sinners, of whom I am chief. And I believe that this is truly thine own immaculate body and this is truly thine own precious blood." Nothing could be clearer. In the Orthodox Church, the presence of Christ in the Sacrament is regarded as a holy mystery that defies human explanation. It is simply a matter of faith. This is true of all the sacraments.

Orthodox Spirituality

There are differences between the Catholic Church and the Orthodox Church. I would suggest that each has its own spiritual orientation. At the beginning of the public life of Christ, at his Baptism in the Jordan, God was revealed as a Trinity of three Persons, the Father, Son, and Holy Spirit. In the Liturgy of St John Chrysostom we pray, "We have seen the true Light, we have received the heavenly Spirit, we have found the true faith, worshipping the undivided Trinity." This short prayer expresses the most important element in Orthodox spirituality, the worship of the Trinity.

While this may seem obvious, it does differ from Catholic spirituality in one fundamental way. Catholic theology and Catholic spirituality begin with "God one in essence." The most important Catholic theologian, Thomas Aquinas, begins his *Summa Theologica* with proofs for the existence of God, not with the Trinity. Orthodoxy begins with the Trinity and bases its spirituality on man's relationship with the Three

Persons of the Godhead. Orthodox spirituality has as its goal the deification of man and his union with God. As Fr Dumitru Stăniloae states, "It has as a basic conviction the existence of a personal God, who is the supreme source of radiating love."[5] Western theology has emphasized the essence of God rather than the Persons of the Trinity.

As a child I was taught to be a good person, obey the commandments of God, go to church, pray, and hope to spend eternity with God in heaven. In Orthodoxy we believe that our destiny is to be united to the Tri-Personal God—already in this life. This process is called divinization or *theosis*. This is possible because God has extended His life into what the Fathers have called the "energies" of God. The importance of Orthodox spirituality was recognized back in the 1930s by the German Catholic theologian Georg Koepgen, who, when speaking of this Trinitarian-based spirituality said, "this spirituality has been most faithfully preserved in the Eastern Church, because she alone has kept in the most unchanged

[5] Dumitru Stăniloae, *Orthodox Spirituality: A Practical Guide for the Faithful and a Definitive Manual for the Scholar*, trans. Archimandrite Jerome (Newville) and Otilia Kloos (South Canaan, PA: St Tikhon's Seminary Press, 2003); Kindle edition, location 828.

way the biblical teaching about the Trinity and its central place in Christian Spirituality."[6]

If I might add a personal note, throughout my life, when I used the word "God," it did not seem to have "content." Even proofs for the existence of God seemed philosophic and even vague. If asked today whether I believe in God, I would answer, "Yes, I believe in God because I first believe in Christ." It is Christ who reveals the Father to us, not some philosopher. In my entire life of faith, the Trinity, although the greatest of mysteries, is far more "understandable" than the concept of "God." My faith is Christ-centered. I believe that some have become atheists because they wrestle with the existence of God. They don't realize that they should begin with the Trinity.

Christian life is a matter of God's grace (His energies) and human freedom. It is a lifetime of prayer and contemplation, of asceticism and mysticism, of receiving the sacraments. It begins with Baptism, which begins the process of divinization, and ends with union with God in His Kingdom. By

---

[6] Georg Koepgen, *Die Gnosis des Christentums* (Salzburg: Verlag Otto Müller, 1939), quoted in Stăniloae, *Orthodox Spirituality*, Kindle edition, location 837.

focusing on the Persons of the Trinity, Orthodox spirituality becomes "very personal."

At the beginning of this book I asked the question, "What does this have to do with the Eucharist?" The question is as important today as it was fifty years ago when I was ordained. The Eucharist is the sacrament of the Kingdom of God. Unlike paraliturgical services, it is our central act of worship. Nothing is more important. Tragically, Catholic churches are being closed across the country by the bishops. One of the reasons is the lack of priests. In the present situation the Eucharist depends upon the availability of celibate men. Is celibacy more important that the Eucharist? Amidst all the discussions about the need for clergy, the issues of lay ministers, women priests, or homosexual priests come up. But the subject of the ordination of married men is quietly avoided. Here there is a strange convergence of three sacraments: the Eucharist, Holy Orders, and Matrimony. No celibates—no priests; no priests—no churches—no Eucharist.

The refusal to ordain married men means fewer priests. The Orthodox Church has both married priests and celibate priests. In the past twenty years the Catholic Archdiocese of Detroit has closed over 100 parishes. Since Vatican II 25,000 priests in the United States have left the priesthood. These problems seem insurmountable in today's Catholic Church. The answer lies in the fact that only one person in the world can do anything about it, the pope.

My Choice of Orthodoxy

Forty years ago, I made the choice of leaving the Church of Rome for the Orthodox Church. This may sound strange, but I believe that I am still part of the One, Holy, Catholic, and Apostolic Church. The decision to become part of the Orthodox Church was not made suddenly. My first memory of the Orthodox Church goes back to my eighth-grade class when our teacher told us that unlike the Protestants, the Orthodox Church has real bishops and real priests, and has valid sacraments. Although I knew nothing about Orthodoxy, this gave me a positive attitude toward Orthodoxy.

Another event occurred in the late 1950s. This event had an indirect but positive influence on my later decision to become Orthodox. One evening my widowed father came home after spending an evening with friends. He told me that they had been to church. It was a Catholic Church but a very different one. He told me that the Mass was in English. The priest gave Communion from a chalice containing the consecrated Bread and Wine. And most surprising of all, the priest was married. My father really enjoyed the service and felt very positive about the entire experience. He had been to an Eastern Rite Catholic Divine Liturgy. All this from a back pew, confession once a month, Irish Catholic. I don't think that he could ever have imagined that his son and grandson would both be celebrating that same Divine Liturgy as married priests. My father died in 1961. The fact that he had this reaction to his experience of Eastern Christianity has been something very positive in my life.

Another influence was my seminary experience. We were taught the history of the Church in which the Eastern Christians were of paramount importance in the clarification of the doctrines of the Church. I also had a roommate who was quite knowledgeable about Orthodoxy. At that point in my life I had a general understanding of the East at least for the first thousand years of the Church.

When I was ordained in 1969 I had a positive outlook about the future of the Catholic Church. Among the memories of my ordination day, one little event stands out. I asked my six-year-old niece, who was attending the parish grade school, what she was learning in catechism class. She replied, "We felt rocks!" Had I been a more insightful person, I might have seen this as sign of the rocks and shoals that lay ahead for the Barque of St Peter.

Although there were many little things that I disliked about what was going on in the Church, I had no thought of abandoning ship. That would come during the time I spent in Rhodesia. I served there from 1973 to 1979. Rhodesia was undergoing a civil war. Although I was never in danger, our bishop and a number of missionaries were killed.

A more significant event occurred my first year in Rhodesia. I became very ill and spent three months in the hospital. Only later did I learn that I was critically ill. Being confined to a bed for three months gives one time to think about one's life. Although I did not entertain thoughts of radically changing my life, I felt that my life could not really go on as it was. I returned to the States, where I discovered that I did not wish to remain in the American Catholic Church. I could not point to one specific thing that I found difficult—it was the whole spirit of the times in the American Catholic Church. I returned to Africa.

Upon returning to Rhodesia, I was given the responsibility of forming a training program for men wishing to become deacons. This was in addition to being pastor of a parish. Most of the men in the program were married.

As the war went on, a number of missionaries were killed. There was a sense of urgency in the diocese that the Church needed *lay* teachers and *lay* baptizers to meet the pastoral needs of the people. What had been something extraordinary—that is, baptism by a lay person—was now becoming something ordinary. Today lay people are doing everything with the exception of consecrating the Eucharist.

No thought was given to the deacons. Why, I wondered? What would prevent the deacons from being ordained to the priesthood? I had heard that in parts of Africa some bishops proposed the ordination of married men. I was aware that in the American Church vocations had fallen off dramatically. I did not realize just how desperate things would become in the States and in Europe.

One very serious theological issue was staring me in the face. The Church professed that the Eucharist was the central act of worship. Nothing could replace it. And yet the people were being deprived of the Eucharist because of the lack of priests. This was true across the Catholic Church. Was celibacy more important to the life of the Church than the Eucharist? It certainly looked that way. Celibacy was a charism, a gift of the Holy Spirit. Can the charism of celibacy be demanded of every priest?

During the final three years of my stay in Rhodesia I lived in a rectory by myself. This was a new experience for me. I had always lived in a religious community of men. I found living alone very difficult. In Orthodoxy monasticism is seen as a charism. Those who leave the community and live a life of solitude are the exception. I was becoming very depressed. I was finding it very difficult to continue as a celibate priest. All these issues brought me to a crisis point. I asked to leave Africa and return to the States. I could not resolve these problems in Africa. By that time I had met a fellow missionary from Austria who I believed would make a very capable clergy wife. We came to a decision to return home and discover whether we both could have an active life in the Orthodox Church. Having an active life for both of us in the Church was of great importance. If this had not been possible, I am not sure what decisions we might have made. St Paul affirms that priesthood and marriage are completely compatible (1 Timothy 3). As things turned out, the doors to Orthodoxy were open to us. The Orthodox people embraced both of us in our parish life.

Upon returning home I began to read about Orthodoxy in the twentieth century. What I discovered was that modern Orthodoxy was still the very same Church that I had studied in the seminary. As I became aware of just how important a role Tradition played in the life of Orthodoxy, I finally real-ized why the Catholic Church had lost so much and why it was in such a confused state.

Later that year I approached an Orthodox archbishop of the Patriarchate of Antioch. I had studied enough about the Orthodox Church to know that what had been abandoned in the Catholic Church was still very much present in the Orthodox Church.

The archbishop was willing to accept me as a mar-ried priest in his jurisdiction. The door was opened. Hav-ing entered Orthodoxy, my wife and I were married in the Orthodox Church. I had the opportunity to spend a year at an Orthodox seminary where I had the experience of studying under some of the finest Orthodox scholars. During the fol-lowing years I served as pastor of several Orthodox parishes.

We now have two adult sons, one of whom is an Ortho-dox priest. The other is also a seminary graduate but has not yet asked to be ordained. Like every life, mine has had its ups and downs, but in retrospect the past forty years have been fruitful. My wife has been a very important part of my parish ministry. We have had a very happy marriage.

I made this choice over forty years ago. Let me say emphatically that I am most grateful for all that I received from the Catholic Church. My faith, my life of worship, and my theological education—all were gifts from my Catholic upbringing. I am not bitter in any way toward the Catholic Church. But I am sad.

At the beginning of this writing, I stated that my intention was not to proselytize. My purpose was to present the Orthodox Church as the apostolic Church containing the fullness of the life of the Church as a haven of faith for those who can no longer be part of Western Christianity. To you who seek such a spiritual home, I suggest that you prayerfully find an Orthodox parish and meet with the priest for guidance in your spiritual journey.

Afterword

Orthodox parishes in North America were founded, as were Catholic and Protestant Churches, by immigrant peoples. The Orthodox Churches, unlike other churches, remained linked to their homeland Churches. This is why you will see Greek Orthodox, Russian Orthodox, Serbian Orthodox, and Antiochian Orthodox Churches in many American cities. Some of these churches retain the liturgical language of their homeland Churches, but most use English in their services. There is also the Orthodox Church in America, founded in the late 1700s as a mission of the Russian Orthodox Church and now self-governing, and normally using English in its services. For those seeking a parish I would suggest calling the parish and asking whether they use English in their services. You might ask if they welcome visitors. Many have websites that can tell you a lot about the church and its history. If you do this, you will avoid "church shopping," a practice where people try to find a church that "suits their needs." Most importantly, ask for the guidance of the Holy Spirit.

Suggested Reading

Thomas Hopko, *The Orthodox Faith*, revised edition, in four volumes: 1. *Doctrine and Scripture*; 2. *Worship*; 3. *Church History*; 4. *Spirituality* (Yonkers, NY: St Vladimir's Seminary Press, 2018). The work was originally published in the 1980s by the Department of Religious Education of the Orthodox Church in America.

John Meyendorff, *Living Tradition* (Crestwood, NY: St Vladimir's Seminary Press, 1978).

Alexander Schmemann, *The Historical Road of Eastern Orthodoxy* (Crestwood, NY: St Vladimir's Seminary Press, 1997).

Alexander Schmemann, *For the Life of the World* (Yonkers, NY: St Vladimir's Seminary Press, 1963; rev. d. 2018).

Timothy Ware, *The Orthodox Church: An Introduction to Eastern Christianity* (London: Pelican Books, 1963; new edition: Penguin Random House UK, 2015).

Metropolitan Kallistos (Timothy) Ware, *The Orthodox Way* (Crestwood NY: St Vladimir's Seminary Press, 1979; revised edition, 2018).

Endorsements

"Fr Daniel Daly's book—on our faith and a review of church history, along with a reflection on Western Christian historical development and doctrine—is a compelling read: well written and intellectually available and usable. It would be perfect for someone to take to university or college, or to a new work assignment. As our young people try to order their own lives in a culturally chaotic time, they will find a reference point in this book, an anchor that helps them weather the storm."

—Bishop Anthony (Michaels)
Antiochian Orthodox Christian Archdiocese of North America

"This book offers a personal witness to Jesus Christ that meets the real needs of real people. There are gems of the Christian Tradition here for everyone. May God crown this effort with His glory."

—Bishop John (Abdalah)
Antiochian Orthodox Christian Archdiocese of North America

"By the grace of God, Fr Daniel Daly wrote *The Choice of Orthodoxy*. While the book is intended for Roman Catholics who may sense loss or emptiness from ceaseless changes, it appeals to every Christian who may feel the church of their childhood has left them. Fr Daniel's keen insight into the loss of Holy Tradition as the source of confusion is absolutely correct. The Lord has revealed Himself to us in the Holy Scriptures (and He does not change), which are a part of a much broader Tradition, from which we must understand them. All that Fr Daniel discusses in his book points us to Christ, who is *the same yesterday, today, and forever* (Heb 13.8). Hopefully, those who read this book will be inspired to further investigate and study the unchanging truths still found within the holy Orthodox Church. While the world around us seems disoriented and confused, as Christians, we need the Christ of the Church as our unchanging point of reference."

—Archbishop Mark (Maymon)
Orthodox Church in America